DATE DUE

MAR 2 8 2003			
GAYLORD		PRINTED IN U.S.A.	

GAYLORD S

Michigan

AMERICA THE BEAUTIFUL
second series

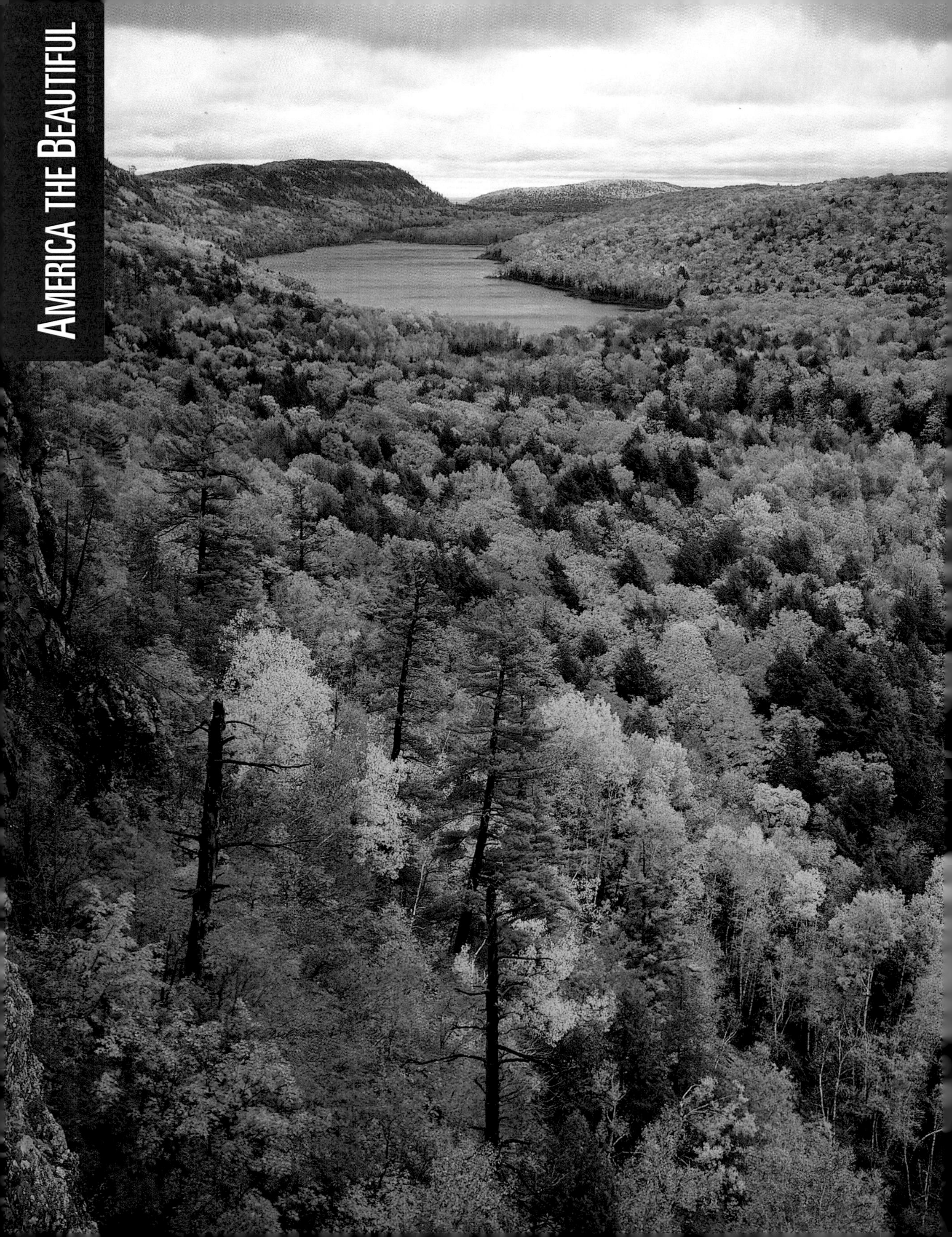

Michigan

Martin Hintz

Children's Press®
A Division of Grolier Publishing
New York   London   Hong Kong   Sydney
Danbury, Connecticut

To the *voyageurs* and the Original People who met them in
what would become Michigan.

Frontispiece: The Porcupine Mountains in autumn

Front cover: Near Grand Portal Point on Lake Superior

Back cover: The Renaissance Center, Detroit

Consultant: Jean S. Bolley, Children's Services, Clarence H. Rosa Library, Lansing,
Michigan

Please note: All statistics are as up-to-date as possible at the time of publication.

Visit Children's Press on the Internet at http://publishing.grolier.com

Book production by Editorial Directions, Inc.

Library of Congress Cataloging-in-Publication Data

Hintz, Martin.
    Michigan / by Martin Hintz.
      p. cm. — (America the beautiful. Second series)
    Includes bibliographical references (p.) and index.
    Summary: Describes the geography, plants, animals, history, economy, language,
religions, culture, sports, art, and people of the state of Michigan.
    ISBN 0-516-20636-2
    1. Michigan — Juvenile literature. [1. Michigan.] I. Title. II. Series.
F566.3.H56 1998
977.4—dc21   97-40669
                                                       CIP
                                                        AC

Acknowledgments

The author wishes to thank the dozens of Michiganders he has met over the years who have helped in countless large and small ways to make this book a success. Among them are the staffs of the Michigan Department of Natural Resources Information Services Center; the Michigan Department of State; the Michigan Bureau of History; the Departments of Agriculture, Education, and Commerce; the Michigan Council for the Arts; and all the tourism officials on the state, county, and community levels.

The author would especially like to thank Al Sandner, Bob Helwig, Doris Scharfenberg, Dixie Franklin, Don Adams, and Kathy Usitalo for their support and encouragement. A nod also goes to President Gerald R. Ford for his commentary on what it was like growing up in Michigan.

State capitol

The Mackinac Bridge

Young Michiganders

Contents

Robin

CHAPTER ONE   Something for Everyone..........................8

CHAPTER TWO   Stepping Toward Today.........................14

CHAPTER THREE   Growing-up Years...................................26

CHAPTER FOUR   Into the Future 38

CHAPTER FIVE   Natural Michigan 50

CHAPTER SIX   Distinctive Cities..................................64

CHAPTER SEVEN   Michigan's Politics................................76

Mackinac Island

A bicycle race

Spirit of Detroit

CHAPTER EIGHT   Michigan's Many Muscles 86

CHAPTER NINE   People Potpourri 98

CHAPTER TEN   The Lively Arts and Athletics 112

Timeline 126

Fast Facts 128

To Find Out More 136

Index 138

Antique Ford

CHAPTER ONE

Something for Everyone

A hiker in Huron National Forest

Michigan is a state that pleases the senses, no matter what the season. Spring brings soft breezes to daffodil-covered hills. Summer nights are bright with stars. Woodsmoke sharpens autumn afternoons. And homemade apple cider tastes so good on frosty winter mornings.

Michigan is an adventure. It is taking a bus down a busy Lansing street or quietly riding past the ancient pine trees near Copper Harbor. It is silent forests and bustling cities. It is the soaring music of Interlochen Arts Academy and the cheers at a Pistons game. It is white-knuckle kayaking on the Michigamme River and brass bands playing at Fort Mackinac.

Natural Michigan

The state explodes with color—from the dazzling floral clock on Belle Isle to the crisp new snow on Porcupine Mountains. Vibrant Picasso canvases and brilliant Chinese ceramics brighten the exhibit halls at the University of Michigan Museum of Art.

Michigan is tall. Detroit's Renaissance Center office and hotel complex soars 73 stories into the sky and the world's largest cedar tree towers 90 feet (27 m) over the Valley of the Giants, along Sleeping Bear Dunes National Lakeshore. You can see Toledo, 30 miles (48 km) away, from the sky tower at Detroit's Boblo Island amusement park.

Opposite: Daffodils bloom in the spring.

And Michigan is deep. You can descend 1 mile (1.6 km) into the earth in the old copper mines of the Keweenaw Peninsula. But be sure to bring a flashlight.

Michigan is powerful, too. Rushing water pours over the spectacular Upper Tahquamenon Falls, the second-largest waterfall east of the Mississippi.

Michigan is long. Take a hike on the North Country Scenic Trail. It's part of a scenic 3,200-mile (5,150-km) walkway linking New York and North Dakota.

The Upper Tahqua-
menon Falls is the
second-largest
waterfall east of
the Mississippi.

Watery Boundaries

Pretend you are in a spaceship looking down at Michigan's zigzag boundaries. The borders are formed by the largest concentration of fresh water in North America. No other state is touched by so many of the Great Lakes. The waters of Superior, Michigan, Huron, and Erie tickle Michigan's in-and-out shoreline.

Now look at a map of Michigan and see the Upper Peninsula and the Lower Peninsula. No other state is divided like this. The split resulted from fancy political footwork in the

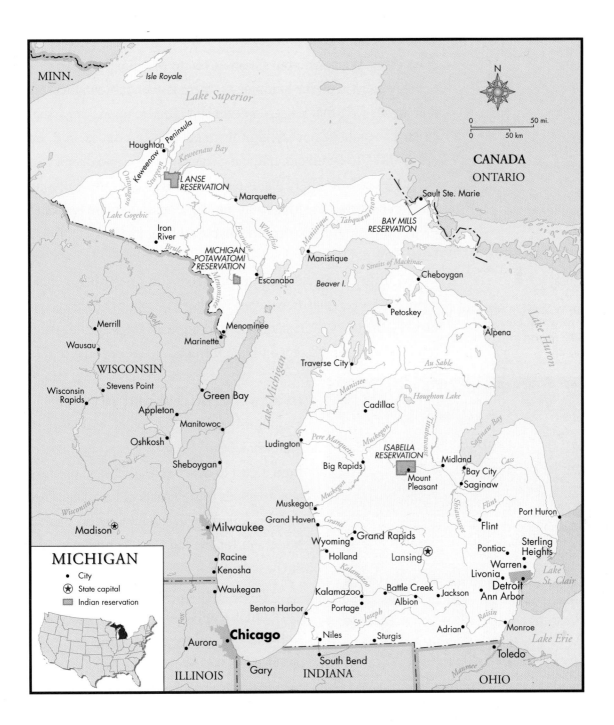

MINN.

Isle Royale

Lake Superior

N

0   50 mi.

0   50 km

CANADA
ONTARIO

Houghton
Keweenaw Peninsula
Keweenaw Bay

Sturgeon
Ontonagon

L'ANSE
RESERVATION

Marquette

Sault Ste. Marie

BAY MILLS
RESERVATION

Lake Gogebic

Iron
River

Escanaba

Whitefish

Tahquamenon

Manistique

Straits of Mackinac

Brule

MICHIGAN
POTAWATOMI
RESERVATION

Escanaba

Manistique

Cheboygan

Beaver I.

Petoskey

Menominee

Merrill

Menominee

Alpena

Lake Huron

Wausau

Marinette

Wolf

WISCONSIN

Traverse City

Au Sable

Manistee

Stevens Point

Cadillac

Houghton Lake

Wisconsin
Rapids

Appleton

Green Bay

Lake Michigan

Ludington

Pere Marquette

Muskegon

Tittabawasse

Manitowoc

ISABELLA
RESERVATION

Midland

Cass

Oshkosh

Big Rapids

Mount
Pleasant

Bay City

Saginaw

Sheboygan

Muskegon

Saginaw Bay

Wisconsin

Muskegon

Grand

Shiawassee

Flint

Port Huron

Madison

Grand Haven

Flint

Milwaukee

Wyoming

Grand Rapids

Pontiac

Sterling
Heights

Racine

Holland

Lansing

Warren

Kenosha

Kalamazoo

Livonia

Detroit

*Lake
St. Clair*

Waukegan

Kalamazoo

Battle Creek

Albion

Jackson

Ann Arbor

Benton Harbor

Portage

St. Joseph

Raisin

Adrian

Monroe

Chicago

Niles

Sturgis

Lake Erie

Aurora

Fox

South Bend

Toledo

ILLINOIS

Gary

INDIANA

Maumee

OHIO

MICHIGAN

- • City
- ⊛ State capital
- ▪ Indian reservation

1800s when the state borders were being drawn. The territory was claimed by Wisconsin but finally given to Michigan instead.

Now zero in on the landscape—there is even more to this state. Geologists joke that if you can't find "it" in Michigan, "it" doesn't exist. The state has everything from peaks, sand dunes, and towering cliffs, to farmland, flatlands, roaring rivers, and deep lakes.

Scientists who study plants enjoy the state's diversity. Lilies and buttercups flower the hills in spring while prairie grasses grace the gentle hills. Autumn colors the maples, birch, and oaks with scarlet and gold. Dark stands of spruce trees are outlined in the snow.

Wildlife managers are excited about the gray wolves, black bears, and deer that now roam Michigan's woods. Eagles, wild turkeys, thrushes, Canada geese, and finches live there too. Perch, rainbow trout, and sturgeon glide through the lakes and rivers.

The gray wolf is among the many species of wildlife found in Michigan.

Industry and Agriculture

Economists praise the state's wide-ranging industrial base. From autos to appliances, from cereal to cybertech, Michigan produces quality goods for international markets. Business leaders from around the world come to Michigan for the latest in technology—and the best deals.

Agricultural experts brag about Michigan's crops—apples and carrots, blueberries and cherries. Eighty-five thousand sheep produce 658,000 pounds (298,460 kg) of wool per year, and chickens contribute more than

1.3 billion eggs. Michigan's hog production totals 450 million pounds (204 million kg).

Many Michiganders

And then there are the people. Their heritage may be German, Polish, Dutch, African, Arabic, Greek, Finnish, Irish, Salvadoran, or Turkish. They speak English, Japanese, Spanish, or any of 100 other languages. They eat hamburgers, pasties, matzos, sushi, tamales, or gyros. They wear blue jeans and saris, turbans and baseball caps, sandals and dress shoes. They watch movies, read novels, visit museums, walk their dogs, and brush their cats. But no matter how they look, what they wear, or what they do for fun, they are all Michiganders.

Michiganders know there is something for everyone here.

Many families enjoy a walk in the Michigan woods.

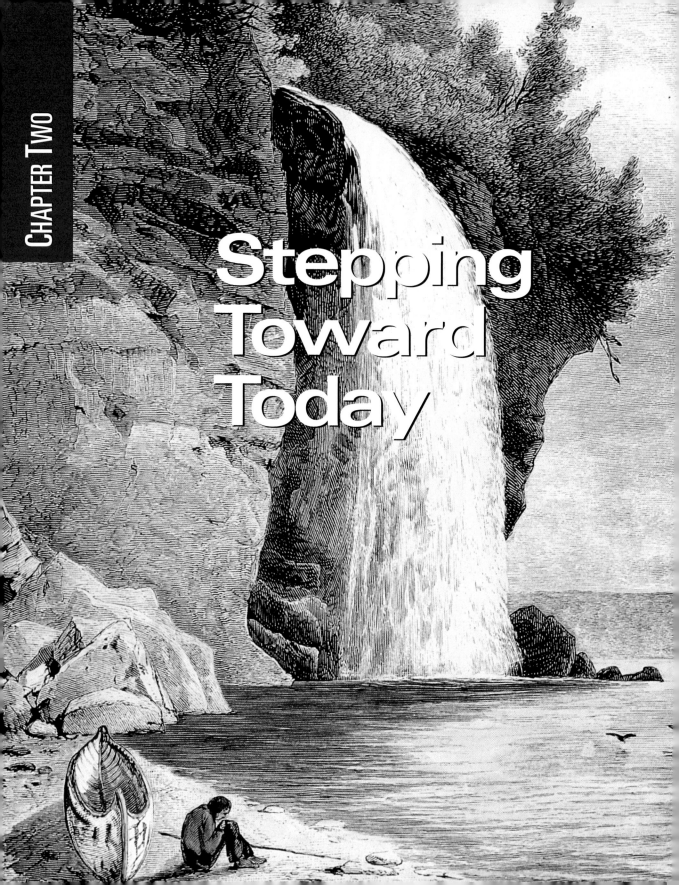

CHAPTER TWO

Stepping Toward Today

A raw wind whistled around the low hills, causing a group of hunters to take shelter under a grove of pine trees. The day was bitter cold, with heavy snow starting to fall. The shivering men pulled their fur robes close around them. They had been on the trail of a big bull elk for hours, following the animal across the rolling, rocky landscape. Their freezing hands held flint-tipped spears. Faced with the gathering darkness, they decided to go back empty-handed. Later, they sat around a campfire with their women and children eating what little food they had left. Someone tossed the bones of a rabbit to one side. They had no way of knowing that Michigan archaeologists would find the remains of their primitive encampment almost ten thousand years later.

Archaeologists dig for Native American relics near Newport, Michigan.

Early Michigan

The ancestors of these first Michiganders were probably hunters who crossed the frozen Bering Strait between Asia and North America during the last Ice Age. As the glaciers covering this region slowly retreated, the people survived by hunting mastodons and other huge beasts. As the climate warmed, descendants of these early people spread out and settled down. In addition to hunting and fishing, they gradually learned to farm the land. The early residents of Michigan lived well. They grew

Opposite: A Native American along the shore of Lake Superior

squash, maize (corn), and other vegetables, and they gathered nuts, berries, and herbs.

Centuries passed, and the groups of people came and went. Native Americans were living in what is now Michigan long before the Europeans arrived in the 1600s. Probably about 100,000 Indians roamed the forests of the Upper Peninsula. Most belonged to the Algonquin language group, including the Ojibwa (Chippewa) and Menominee. Other tribes lived in the Lower Peninsula, including the Miami, Ottawa, and Potawatomi. A small group of Wyandot, who spoke the Iroquois language, settled around what is now Detroit.

By this time, most of Michigan was covered with forests of pine and oak trees up to 100 feet (30 m) high. It was said that a squirrel could travel the entire length of the state without touching the ground! The Native Americans left no mark on the landscape as they traveled through these thick forests. Though they did not have an easy life, they were in tune with their environment, and they lived well.

In the mid-1600s, change was on the way. Explorers came from New France (Canada). They were sent by Samuel de Champlain, governor of Quebec, to find the fabled Northwest Passage, a direct route to the Pacific Ocean. A direct route would lead to the riches of China and make it easier to transport goods back to Europe. Étienne Brulé, who explored the Upper Peninsula around 1620, was probably the first European to visit Michigan.

In 1634, Jean Nicolet sailed through the Straits of Mackinac into Lake Michigan. When he stepped ashore near Green Bay, Wisconsin, Nicolet thought he had reached China. To mark the occasion, he wore a colorful silk robe. The Indians who greeted Nicolet were definitely impressed, but they had never heard of China.

Mission Established

A Jesuit missionary named René Ménard established a mission at Keweenaw Bay, on the tip of the Upper Peninsula, in 1660. Eight years later, Sault Ste. Marie—Michigan's first permanent settlement—was founded by Father Jacques Marquette and other priests followed. It was difficult to convert the Indians to Christianity, considering the language and cultural barriers, but the French missionaries tried hard.

Principal Street in Sault Ste. Marie, Michigan's first permanent settlement

Marquette meets the Native Americans.

Exploration of Michigan

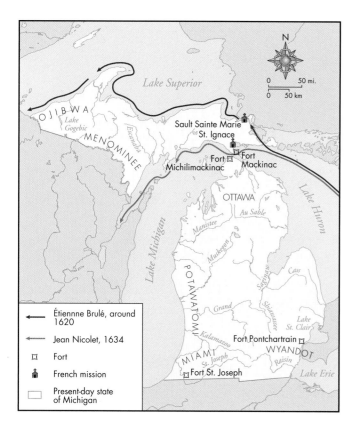

By the 1700s, the French had explored much of the region and mapped many of the surrounding lakes and rivers. They built forts, missions, and trading posts in both the Upper and Lower Peninsulas. Many married Indian women and raised families. In 1701, Antoine de la Mothe Cadillac founded Fort Pontchartrain, a tiny outpost that eventually became the sprawling city of Detroit.

Trading Furs

Through these years, European demand for furs soared. The Indians eagerly traded beaver, mink, fox, and other fur pelts for cloth, iron pots, hatchets, guns—and alcohol. They soon came to rely on Europeans for most of their needs, often abandoning their traditional ways of life. When the numbers of animals decreased in one area, the Indians had to move farther west. This caused trouble with the Indians already living there.

The name *voyageurs* was given to a group of daring French-Canadians who paddled their canoes deep into Indian territory. As they cruised along, they sang about the forests, women, and home. They brought furs back to Quebec City and Montreal. The pelts were then sent to Europe, where they were made into hats and other clothing. This trade flourished for 200 years.

The profits to be made in the fur business soon brought competitors. The British also wanted some of the money that could be made. Competition between the French and British was one cause of the Seven Years' War that broke out in 1756 in Europe. The war affected much of North America, forcing American Indian tribes to choose sides. Life on the frontier became even more dangerous as the Europeans and their Indian allies fought among themselves. However, with the defeat of the French in 1763, the British gained control over most of North America. Michigan was part of that prize.

Pontiac speaking with his people

Pontiac's War

When the French lost the war, Pontiac, chief of the Ottawa, decided he was tired of Europeans interfering in the lives of his people. He gathered many other tribes under his leadership and fought back. In what became known as Pontiac's War, his warriors massacred the British garrison at Fort Michilimackinac, now Mackinaw City. Other outposts were also attacked, villages were burned, and settlers were killed by the angry Indians. Detroit remained under siege for nearly seven months before Pontiac gave up and moved on. Fortunately, this bloody battle

A trading post, where furs and other items were exchanged

Pontiac, Ottawa Chief

Pontiac, a natural leader, was born about 1720. He was an ally of the French and feared the aggressive British expansion. In 1762, he organized the Pontiac Alliance, which united Native American tribes from the Great Lakes to the Gulf of Mexico. The Pontiac Alliance pledged to drive out the British west of the Allegheny Mountains. The Pontiac Alliance was the greatest union of American Indian nations ever mounted against the whites in North America.

When the Indians' widespread attack was launched in May 1763, the entire frontier was enveloped in flames. But European firepower overcame Pontiac's warriors and he was forced to negotiate a peace treaty. In 1769 in Illinois, Pontiac was murdered by another Indian. Pontiac is said to be buried on Apple Island, near Pontiac, Michigan, the city that was named for him.■

was the last major confrontation between Michigan's Native Americans and the European newcomers.

The British were more interested in fur trading than in settling the region, but the conflicts of that time did not allow them to accomplish much of either. The American Revolutionary War began soon afterward, lasting for eight long and bloody years. And while the British were fighting the American colonists, they also found themselves in a fierce war with Spain.

Spanish Attack

In 1781, Spanish forces penetrated deep into North America and captured Fort St. Joseph, the British stronghold that is now Niles, Michigan. The Spanish were able to hold the fort for only one day before being driven out. Niles residents now proudly say that their town is the only community in Michigan where the flags of France, England, Spain, and the United States have all flown.

In 1783, the British gave up the colonial war. However, British traders continued their Michigan fur business for another thirteen years. They finally surrendered Detroit and Fort Mackinac in 1796.

Northwest Territory Formed

In 1787, Michigan was included in the Northwest Territory. This was the new name given to a vast area of lakes, forests, and flora and fauna across the upper midwestern states of Michigan, Ohio, Indiana, Illinois, Wisconsin, and sections of eastern Minnesota. However, some of Michigan's original land was given to the Indiana Territory established by Congress in 1800. Three years later, all of Michigan was included in that territory.

In 1805, Congress established the Territory of Michigan, which included the Lower Peninsula and the eastern part of the Upper Peninsula. All these changing boundaries were very confusing to the people on the Michigan frontier, but most of them did not care who was in charge, as long as they were left alone.

The British troops recapture Detroit in the War of 1812.

Conflict then erupted again between Great Britain and the young United States. During the War of 1812, British troops recaptured Detroit and Fort Mackinac. In a bloody seesaw, the Americans regained Detroit the following year. After peace was declared in 1814, the British lowered their flag and returned Fort Mackinac. That was the last time a foreign flag flew over Michigan.

Treaties Signed

Treaties with American Indians were signed in 1819, 1821, and 1836. By 1840, most of the first inhabitants of Michigan had been

Historical map of Michigan

Henry Rowe Schoolcraft preserved many Native American legends

forced onto reservations farther west. It would be generations before there was another strong presence of Native Americans in Michigan. Henry Rowe Schoolcraft, a famous Michigan writer and educator in the 1800s, preserved many Indian legends and wrote about Native Americans' way of life. His tales give insights into how Michigan's first residents survived.

Newcomers to Michigan

Now that the frontier was quiet, Michigan was due for more changes. In 1825, the 363-mile (584-km) Erie Canal was completed in New York state. The waterway linked the Great Lakes with the Atlantic Ocean and this created a much quicker route between the eastern states and western territories. Settlers no longer had to travel overland on poor roads, facing bad weather, robbers, and broken-down wagons. The canal barges shortened the trip to several weeks. Thousands of newcomers took advantage of this "modern" mode of transportation. They flocked to the newly opened farmland. They were eager to put down roots. Michigan's population tripled in just a few years.

Once they reached Detroit, however, the pioneers again faced a rough journey over poor roads. The bumpy Chicago Trail led settlers west around the bottom of Lake Michigan into Illinois. Others moved on to the Lower Peninsula. In their letters home, they praised Michigan's fertile soil and clean water and attracted even more newcomers. Most of these new settlers came from New England.

Statehood Sought

Under the terms of the Northwest Ordinance (the laws governing the Northwest Territory), a region within the territory could seek statehood if 60,000 people lived there. Most Michiganders were interested in pursuing statehood, so their representatives got together to discuss the best way to proceed. Helping lead the way was Stevens T. Mason. He was only nineteen when he was appointed acting territorial secretary. Mason authorized a census to count the number of Michiganders and be sure there were the required number of people. In 1834, at age twenty-two, Mason was elected the first territorial governor.

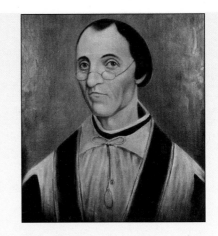

Father Gabriel Richard

Father Gabriel Richard (*Ree-SHARD*), the pastor of St. Anne's Church in Detroit, was the only Catholic priest in the U.S. Congress for more than 100 years. The French-born priest was elected in 1823 and served for two years. In a tight race, he received the support of his French-speaking parishioners, who made up most of the voting population. Not until 1970 did another priest sit in Congress. He was Father Robert Drinan of Massachusetts. ■

Under Mason's firm hand, a state constitution was drawn up and ratified, or approved, on October 5, 1835. Admission to the Union was delayed by Congress, however, because of a dispute between the Michigan Territory and the state of Ohio over a small strip of land near Toledo, Ohio. Both sides sent their militia to the area and there was much marching around and shouting. But no shots were fired in the dispute, which lasted from 1835 to 1837. To settle the argument, Congress granted Ohio the Toledo Strip and Michigan was given the entire Upper Peninsula. Not many people in lower

24th Cong[ss]

2. Sep[ss]

In Senate Mes
Dec 29, 1836.

Mr Grundy from the Com: on the Judiciary reported the
following bill, which was read twice and postponed to, and
made the order of the day for Monday the 2 of January next.

A Bill

To admit the State of Michigan into
the Union, upon an equal footing with
the original States.

"Whereas, in pursuance of the act of
Congress, of June the fifteenth, eighteen hundred
and thirty six, entitled "An act to establish
the northern boundary of the State of Ohio,
and to provide for the admission of the State
of Michigan into the Union upon the
conditions therein expressed", a convention of
delegates elected by the people of the said
State of Michigan for the sole purpose of
giving their assent to the boundaries of the
said State of Michigan as described, declared,
and established, in and by the said act,
did, on the fifteenth of December, eighteen
hundred and thirty six, assent to the
provisions of said act ___ Therefore ___

Be it enacted by the Senate and House
of Representatives of the United States of America
in Congress assembled, That the State of
Michigan, shall be one, and is hereby declared
to be one, of the United States of America, and
admitted into the Union, on an equal footing
with the original States in all respects whatever.

The document that
gave Michigan
statehood

Michigan thought the relatively unknown Upper Peninsula was worth much. They wanted to keep the richer farmland of the Toledo Strip, even though it was only 75 miles (121 km) long and between 5 and 8 miles (8 and 13 km) wide. But because most Michiganders eagerly sought statehood, they approved the terms of the agreement.

The way was then clear for Michigan to become the twenty-sixth state of the Union on January 26, 1837. Mason, who was elected the first state governor, ranks as the youngest governor in the history of the state.

Steps Toward Statehood

1834
Stevens T. Mason elected territorial governor

October 5, 1835
State constitution approved

1835–1837
Toledo War land dispute between Michigan and Ohio

January 26, 1837
Michigan becomes a state.

1840
Native Americans give up the last of their claims to land in Michigan. ▩

CHAPTER THREE

Growing-up Years

An immigrant family learning how to grow its own food.

The Republic Iron Mine

After statehood, Michigan grew rapidly. Eager Michiganders were ready to reach out into the bright future. Tens of thousands of settlers flooded the state, looking for prosperity. Many of the newcomers were born overseas. They came from exotic lands and spoke many different languages. Entire families arrived—mothers and fathers, grandparents and babies, sons and daughters. Some children came alone, perhaps looking for relatives who had come ahead of them or simply striking out on their own. Germans, Finns, Dutch, Belgians, English, Irish, Swedes, and others stepped off schooners in Detroit or trekked overland from Ohio.

Even the Upper Peninsula received its share of eager settlers. They were lured to the rockbound landscape by the rich minerals and the timber. Miners dug for copper and iron; boomtowns appeared overnight. When the miners and loggers came to town, the streets were crowded and the saloons were busy with workers seeking entertainment.

Opposite: An elevated view of the Mackinac Bridge

Problems for Michigan

In 1847, the capital of Michigan was moved from Detroit to the more central Lansing. Business flourished around the state as roads improved and the first rail lines were laid. But even with this prosperity, all was not calm and comfortable.

Slavery was a growing problem in the United States at this time. There were loud debates over the pros and cons of human— or inhuman—bondage. The arguments were intense and passions were high. The free state of Michigan could not avoid the gathering storm.

Abolitionists, fervent antislavery people, hid African-Americans who escaped from their masters in the South's slave-holding states. The route the African-Americans took from the Southern plantations to freedom in Canada was called the Underground Railroad. There were several stops on the "railroad" in Michigan. These "safe houses" were hidden in barns, churches, stores, or schools. Michiganders of all religions and political persuasions eagerly helped the frightened, tired, and hungry escapees. Slave-catchers who sought the return of a slaveholder's "property" were sometimes beaten and chased out of Michigan towns.

Civil War Begins

Within a few years, arguments between the North and South turned to gunfire. The Civil War (1861–1865) was the bloodiest conflict in U.S. history. It split the nation between the Union (the North) and the Confederacy (the South). They fought over many issues, from

The Beginning of the Republican Party

Political organizations in the northern states during the 1850s gathered around the banner of antislavery. A group of reformers met on February 28, 1854, in Ripon, Wisconsin, claiming to be the political heirs of the late President Thomas Jefferson and his Democratic-Republican Party.

They believed that Jefferson influenced the writing of the Northwest Ordinance of 1787, which abolished slavery in the territories north of the Ohio River. This area included Michigan, so these "Republicans" felt that they represented the values of the Declaration of Independence, which Jefferson helped to write.

A Michigan state antislavery convention met at Jackson shortly after the Wisconsin gathering. On July 6, 1854, the Michiganders formally adopted the "Republican Party" as their name. Other states quickly followed their lead and today's Republican Party was launched. ■

states' rights to slavery. There was also an economic aspect to the war. The agricultural economy of the South squared off against the North's industrial strength.

Michigan was a major participant on the Union side. The state had thirty-one regiments of infantry, eleven regiments of cavalry, fourteen batteries of artillery, one regiment of sharp-

Michigan's First Infantry under review during the Civil War

shooters, and one regiment of engineers. In addition, many Michigan men joined units from other states. Approximately 90,000 Michiganders served during the war. Of those, 14,434 never returned. Some died of disease or wounds, while others were reported missing in action or were buried in unmarked graves.

General Custer

The famous Michigan Brigade, a cavalry regiment during the Civil War, was led by Brigadier General George Armstrong Custer—a colorful military figure from Monroe, Michigan. Custer was appointed temporary brigadier general of volunteers in 1863 because of his distinguished service in earlier campaigns. He led his troops through the Wilderness and Shenandoah campaigns. Custer was always in the front of the action, helping pursue Confederate General Robert L. Lee of Richmond, the rebel capital. He received Lee's flag of truce, a towel, when the Confederates finally surrendered.

After the Civil War, Custer was made lieutenant colonel of the newly organized Seventh Cavalry. The regiment was active on the frontier, battling the Plains Indians. Never one to listen to advice, stubborn Custer underestimated the strength of the Indians united under Sioux chiefs Sitting Bull and Crazy Horse. He divided his troops into three groups, sending each in different directions. On June 25, 1876, Custer and a few of his men attacked the Indians at the Little Bighorn River in Montana Territory. The Indians outfought the flamboyant general and he was killed. The site is now a national cemetery, established in 1879. A granite monument marks the spot where Custer and his soldiers fell. ■

A Place to Work

After the Civil War, returning veterans were glad for the peace and quiet that awaited them in Michigan. They quickly settled into a daily routine on their farms and in shops, factories, and businesses.

More workers were needed as Michigan's economy exploded after the war. Steamship lines and mining and railroad companies sent agents to Europe to recruit workers and American "fever" spread. People who were accustomed to cramped living conditions and oppressive governments looked upon the United States as the land of opportunity. To them, the streets in America were paved with gold. Of course, vast lands were open to everyone who wanted to claim a piece of ground. And everyone was guaranteed a good job. Naturally, life would be much easier—or so many newcomers thought.

But once the immigrants arrived in Michigan, they discovered there was a lot of hard work ahead. Long hours, little pay, and no benefits confronted the industrial workers. The farmers, miners, and loggers were not much better off. But Michiganders, whether newly arrived immigrants or longtime residents, yearned for a better life. They sent their sons to technical schools to learn a trade. Their daughters went to business colleges to study bookkeeping or that newfangled typing. While office work did not earn as much as factory labor, it had more prestige. At that time, most people believed that a woman should work only until she found a husband to take care of her.

Labor organizations were formed to speak out for the workers. The printers' union, which was started in 1835, affiliated with the

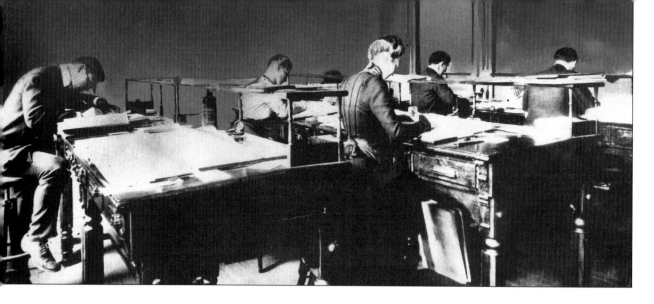

Both men and women worked in offices after the Civil War.

International Typographical Union in 1852. It remains the state's oldest labor group. Then came the stonecutters' union in 1855, the iron molders' in 1860, and the machinists' and blacksmiths' in 1861. The National Brotherhood of Locomotive Engineers was organized in Detroit in 1863. Shoemakers, cigarmakers, harness and collar makers, and laborers also set up unions to protect their interests.

The movement for an eight-hour working day was supported by all these groups, though it was years before such a workday was accepted. At this time, most people worked from ten to twelve hours a day, six days a week. And workers considered themselves lucky to get five dollars a day in wages.

Well after dark, workers dragged themselves home from a long day of hard labor. Then they had to rise before the sun to be sure to be on time for their factory job. Most mothers worked at home. They kept an eye on the children, washed and ironed, cooked and cleaned. It was a hard life for everyone, especially if the family lived in a large city with its pollution, crowded streets and poor sanitation. The labor unions and Michigan's many ethnic societies helped their members to have a decent social life and provided financial assistance during tough times.

Farmers also had a tough time. They had to clear fields, sow crops, and look after livestock. Unlike today's farmers, early Michigan farmers did not have the benefit of giant tractors, milking machines, and other labor-saving devices. Farmers were also at the mercy of the railroads that carried their goods to market and of the banks that lent money—at high interest rates. Many agricultural workers joined the Grange, an organization that was similar to labor unions. The Grange helped them over the rough spots.

Michigan's Knights of Labor helped to get their supporters elected to government positions. Through their efforts, the legislature formed the Michigan Department of Labor in 1883. Labor activists also helped pass a law that kept young people in school until they were sixteen. They then secured approval for a ten-hour working day. In 1887, child labor in Michigan's mines was outlawed and mine-safety provisions were passed. Lumbermen demanding a ten-hour day traveled upriver from the timber town of Saginaw, stopping at each mill to urge workers to strike. Within days, seventy-eight mills were closed and the workers won.

The American Federation of Labor (AFL) made many attempts to organize laborers in the new auto industry after the turn of the

Richard F. Trevellick, Labor Leader

Richard F. Trevellick of Detroit was an early labor leader. In the mid-1860s, he became the first president of the Detroit Trades Assembly and was later elected president of the International Union of Ship Carpenters and Caulkers. He served on many national labor committees, always advocating better working conditions. Trevellick often traveled to Washington, D.C., to lobby for his workers. He was a fearless speaker and organized rousing rallies urging protection of the workers. ■

An assembly line at the Ford Rouge plant in the 1920s

century. Work in auto factories was difficult and dangerous. There were slippery floors, sharp metal fragments, and no protective headgear or gloves. The smoke-filled air was hard to breathe. The fast-paced assembly line was stressful, and there were many accidents. Foremen had the power to hire workers they liked and fire those they did not like. Numerous labor stoppages occurred in the 1920s and early 1930s, many led by the United Auto Workers. In Flint, workers took over the General Motors auto plants for six weeks. They stayed in their factories and slept on car seats. Their wives and friends passed sandwiches and soup to them through the shattered windows of the occupied plants.

Workers Rally

One of the biggest labor actions in Michigan occurred in February 1937. More than 150,000 workers rallied on Detroit's Cadillac Square to support striking Chrysler workers who had taken over their plants. The strikers refused to leave the plants until their demands were met. This "sit-down" strike was one of the major events in U.S. labor history.

In 1937, more than 150,000 people gathered in Detroit's Cadillac Square to support their striking colleagues.

Walter Reuther

It was not easy organizing unions and it was often dangerous. Factory security personnel and local police often attacked labor organizers. One such incident was the famous Battle of the Overpass on May 26, 1937. Private security men at a Ford auto plant attacked United Auto Workers members who were handing out literature. Labor leader Walter Reuther was among those beaten.

Reuther was born in 1907 in West Virginia. His father was an active trade unionist and Socialist candidate for U.S. Congress. Reuther left high school at age fifteen to go to work. By eighteen, he was urging his fellow workers to protest against working on Sunday. He was fired for this activity, so he traveled around the world for almost three years, working as a machinist.

Upon his return to America in 1936, Reuther joined the United Auto Workers. He became vice president of a local chapter in Detroit and helped lead the autoworkers' massive sit-down strikes. Even though he was attacked in the Battle of the Overpass, he continued his labor activities in Michigan and around the United States. Reuther was president of the United Auto Workers from 1946 until his death in 1970 in Pellston, Michigan. ◾

The M-10 "tank destroyer" was mass-produced at General Motors' tank arsenal during World War I.

In War and Peace

In 1917, the United States declared war on Germany and entered World War I (1914–1918). Patriotic excitement led thousands of Michigan men to enlist. Even before the country had entered the war, hundreds had already joined the Canadian army and were fighting in Europe. Unfortunately, some people discriminated against Michiganders of German and Austrian descent and feared their customs. As an example of anti-German hysteria, the word *hamburger* became "liberty sausage" and frankfurters were called "hot dogs" because Hamburg and Frankfurt were German cities.

Of the 135,485 men that Michigan sent to the armed forces during the war, 5,000 died in action and another 15,000 were wounded. But the state's most important contribution to the war effort was its industrial power. Guns, tanks, and other military supplies poured out of Michigan factories. This push set the stage for the next rise in Michigan's economic growth.

Demonstrating Michigan's boom after World War I was the growth of the construction industry in Detroit. Between 1927 and 1928, many of the city's most famous office buildings were erected. Among them were the forty-six-story Penobscot Building, the forty-story New Union Trust Building and the Cadillac Tower, the thirty-eight-story David Stott Building, the twenty-eight-floor Fischer Building, and many others. Construction investment totaled

$200 million in 1927, thirty-three times more than the $6 million spent in 1900.

In those days, labor was cheap and often the value of human life was forgotten. It was just necessary to get the job done, inexpensively and fast. It is estimated that at least one worker was killed for every floor of every building put up during the 1920s.

The Eighteenth Amendment to the U.S. Constitution affected Michigan when it was passed in 1917 and ratified by three-fourths of the states in 1919. The amendment (called Prohibition) outlawed the manufacture and sale of alcohol, a measure that was widely ignored by much of the country. Gangsters moved in to control the market, organizing the smuggling of alcohol across the Detroit River from Canada in speedboats. Mobsters, such as Detroit's infamous Purple Gang, seemed to rule the streets.

These workers line up outside the U.S. Rubber Company in Detroit, having heard rumors that the company was hiring.

Michigan's growth spurt did not last forever, however. By the mid-1930s, the nation was sliding into the Great Depression. While the 1920s were great years for Michigan workers, the next decade was devastating. Banks collapsed; industries closed; hundreds of thousands of people were out of work. As an example, Ford Motor Company employed 128,000 people in 1929. Two years later, the workforce was slashed to 37,000. In an effort to save money, some companies cut wages to $3 a day. Government leaders insisted that there was nothing to worry about, but they were wrong.

Michigan's once bright future became cloudy indeed.

CHAPTER FOUR

Into the
Future

Michigan, like the rest of the United States, was hit hard during the 1930s as the worldwide economic crisis deepened. Parents sold everything they had to buy food for their children. People were evicted from their homes when they could not pay the rent or the mortgage. Hungry families lined up outside soup kitchens for a free meal. The Hungarian Free Kitchen, the Jewish Emergency Relief Fund, and similar private groups desperately tried to keep up.

The state's minority community was hit hardest because it was already at the bottom of the labor ladder. During the Great Depression, unemployment reached 80 percent in some African-American neighborhoods in Detroit. When things seemed to be at their worst, Fannie Peck, wife of a Detroit minister, formed the Housewives' League—the first group designed to deal with the hardships facing black businesswomen and homemakers. Soon, Mrs. Peck was speaking nationally on such issues. On a more militant side, the Black Muslim movement started in Detroit in the 1930s, preaching a black nationalist message.

A soup kitchen during the Great Depression

Life Unravels

Stable community life began to unravel during the Great Depression. Several Michigan towns had to close their fire departments, shut down their electric plants, and enforce other strict money-

Opposite: The Penobscot Building in Detroit

Mighty Joe Louis

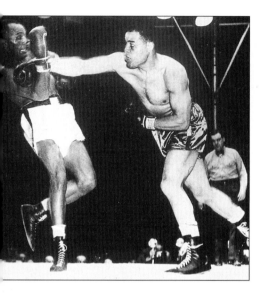

Few people made such a positive impact on Michigan in the 1930s as Joe Louis (left), a boxer from Detroit's East Side. He was born in Alabama and moved north with his family at the age of seven. Louis got his start in the ring by winning the National Amateur Association light-heavyweight championship. He turned professional in 1934 and went on to win twenty-three straight fights, nineteen by knockouts. Louis captured the world heavyweight championship in 1937 and held it for twelve years.

Crowds and reporters followed Louis everywhere, especially in Detroit's African-American neighborhoods. They could forget their troubles for a time as they cheered Louis on to victory after victory. As Louis's career surged ahead, he remained a gentleman and a strong role model for young blacks. Louis retired in 1949 but returned to the ring in 1950, only to lose to the new champion, Ezzard Charles. Yet Louis did not give up. He won eight more fights before being knocked out by Rocky Marciano in 1951. His overall ring record was a stunning sixty-six victories in seventy-one fights, including forty-nine by knockouts. ∎

saving measures. They did not have enough money to keep up these essential services. Police broke up protests over layoffs and pay cuts. Conservative politicians said that unemployment was the workers' problem. They said the jobless were lazy and that any government help would only reward such behavior. That misconception shocked people who had worked all their lives and then were forced out on the street. But there was little they could do.

Some local officials tried desperately to help during the Depression. One such politician was Detroit mayor Frank Murphy. He

Father Charles Coughlin

During the upheaval of the 1930s, people listened to anyone who promised a better future. They wanted a solution to their problems. Father Charles Coughlin (right), a Catholic priest in Detroit, preached on a weekly radio show and published a newspaper. Through these media outlets, he vented the frustration felt by thousands of people across the country. But Coughlin gradually became more and more radical, and he seemed critical of everything.

His angry speeches got him into a great deal of trouble with church and political leaders. Coughlin was told to be quiet or stop being a priest. Faced with these choices, he gave up his radio show and his paper and went back to being a parish priest in Royal Oak, Michigan. ▪

opened up empty warehouses to house the homeless, established food pantries, and promoted gardening as one way to get food.

But this was not enough, and hungry people took to the streets. In Dearborn on March 7, 1931, the police and the Ford Company security personnel fired into a peaceful crowd of unemployed marchers. Four men were killed and a fifth later died of his wounds. No one was ever brought to trial for these killings even though it was shown that the authorities overreacted badly.

The election of Democratic president Franklin Delano Roosevelt in 1932 showed that the nation wanted, and needed, a change in policy. Michigan governor William A. Comstock and many other Democrats were also swept into power in that election. Roosevelt did not hesitate to help the people. With the support of Congress, he set up federal bureaus that provided relief and jobs. On the state level, social welfare programs were established.

B-24 bombers being built at the Willow Run plant in 1943

These were seesaw years, as the Democrats and Republicans battled for political power in Michigan. With President Roosevelt's support, Detroit's former Mayor Frank Murphy was elected governor in 1936. Murphy's negotiating skills helped alleviate much of the tension during the years of labor unrest.

Soon the harsh clouds of war again rolled over Europe as World War II (1939–1945) broke out. In 1941, Roosevelt asked William S. Knudsen, vice president of General Motors, to help prepare America for its eventual entry into the war. Roosevelt knew that Knudsen's managerial skills were valuable.

The United States entered the conflict when Japan attacked Pearl Harbor on December 7, 1941. The auto plants were again turned over to the manufacture of planes, trucks, and weapons. From September 1939 to August 1945, Michigan's industry contributed an estimated $50 billion worth of material to the war effort. A bomber factory at Willow Run—the world's largest assembly plant—cost more than $100 million. When the plant was finally up and running, one new bomber rolled out of its doors every hour.

Workers Rehired

These were boom times again for Michigan. Workers were back on the job. African-Americans were recruited in the South to help in the factories. Between 50,000 and 60,000 blacks migrated to Detroit. At first it was hard to convince employers that blacks were capable of doing the same work as whites. To prod the companies, President Roosevelt outlawed discrimination in the workplace. He said it was the duty of employers and labor organizations to encourage fair hiring practices.

There was a shortage of housing for these new workers, too. As African-Americans sought better living and working conditions, they began to move into previously all-white areas. Fights broke out and people were killed. One of the worst confrontations occurred in June 1943, at the amusement park on Belle Isle, a small island in the Detroit River. This was a city park that was open to both blacks and whites. By the end of the riot, which had spread throughout the city, thirty-four people had died and many more were injured. This incident led community leaders to realize that they had to work harder to defuse racial tension. Gradually, the situation improved, at least on the surface.

African-Americans were not the only newcomers facing challenges during the war years in Michigan. Thousands of white

African-American workers forge a piece of hot metal in the 1950s.

The Beginnings of Motown

Blues singer John Lee Hooker (left) was born in Mississippi and came to Detroit to work in a factory during World War II. Hooker's guitar and his gritty songs captured the migrants' feelings about their changing lives. He left his factory job for good in 1948 and became one of America's great musical artists.

Hooker, jazzman Pepper Adams, percussionist Roy Brooks, trumpeter Donald Byrd, drummer Elvin Jones, and others prepared the ground for the distinctive Motown sound of the 1960s and 1970s. Motown Records featured a mix of gospel, romantic lyrics, and upbeat rhythm. One of the record label's major performers was honey-voiced singer Aretha Franklin, the Queen of Soul. Her father was the Reverend Clarence Franklin, a leader of Detroit's civil right movement in the 1960s. ■

migrants from Kentucky and Tennessee came looking for jobs. Many were not used to the ways of the big city or to the cold northern winters. The locals called the new arrivals "hillbillies" and other insulting nicknames.

Women also enjoyed a larger role in Michigan's industry as they went to work in the big plants. With their husbands fighting overseas, wives needed money to make ends meet. Exhausted, they came home to clean and bake and cook for their children. It was a tough life, even when other family members helped out.

Economy Jolted

The war years marked great social changes in Michigan. And there was a severe jolt to the state's economy immediately after the war. Returning veterans needed jobs, which resulted in layoffs for women and minorities. It took time to retool the weapon plants to produce items needed in peacetime.

The Mackinac Bridge

Mackinaw City had always been a bottleneck for motorists. There vacationers had to ferry their cars across the Straits of Mackinac (pronounced *Mackinaw*) to reach St. Ignace on the opposite shore. During peak holiday times, lines of waiting cars were 20 miles (32 km) long.

After much discussion in the legislature, the state finally decided to build a bridge across the straits in 1954.

The Mackinac Bridge is one of the longest suspension bridges in the world. The central span of the bridge extends 3,800 feet (1,158 m) between the main towers, which soar 552 feet (168 m) above the waterline, allowing large freighters to pass underneath. The total length of the bridge is 26,444 feet (8,060 m). The structure, which weighs more than 1 million tons, cost $90 million to build. ■

The Car Capital

The early 1950s saw a rebirth of the auto industry as suburbs developed around the larger cities. Everyone "had" to have a new car. Michigan's economy increasingly became centered around the automobile, a dependency that would be a problem in decades to come. Michigan became known as a "one-industry" state, with 6 million cars built there in 1956 and even more in following years. Yet not all of Michigan shared in the auto boom.

The Upper Peninsula (UP) was especially hard-hit as the mining industry collapsed. To take up the economic slack, the natural resources of the UP needed to be exploited in a more creative way. Tourism was thought to be one answer. With that in mind, tourism promotion became an important component in marketing the state. The construction of interstate and local highways in the 1950s helped open up new areas of Michigan. Only a few years earlier, it had taken a full day to drive from the heavily populated south to the refreshing getaway areas in the far north. With the expanded highway system, the journey took only a few hours. Today, up to 22 million visitors per year visit Michigan, bringing billions of dollars into the state economy.

To ensure there was a new generation of safe drivers, legislation was passed in 1956 providing driver education in Michigan high schools. It was the first law of its kind in the United States.

Tough Times

The 1960s were years of turmoil for Michigan. A new constitution was needed to update language left from the state's earliest days. It was also time to streamline the state government and courts. In

1963, a statewide vote approved a constitution, the state's fourth such document. The new constitution was geared to the twentieth century rather than the needs of past years.

During the 1960s, the state's economy suffered once again. Faced with competition from overseas automakers, the car industry slumped, and many workers lost their jobs. These were also the Vietnam War years, when Michigan's college campuses were swept up in antiwar protest.

Michigan's African-American citizens were also eager to move ahead economically and socially. Civil rights leader Dr. Martin Luther King Jr. came to Detroit in 1963 and led 125,000 people in

Martin Luther King Jr. (with hand raised) leads a rally in Detroit during his 1963 visit.

a rally urging a nonviolent end to discrimination. Black Muslim organizer Malcolm X, who lived in Lansing as a child, also returned to the state to demand more rights for his people. The African-American community remained frustrated over the lack of good housing and the scarcity of jobs.

All these issues contributed to the worst riot in Detroit's history, which erupted in July 1967. The Michigan National Guard had to be called in to restore order. When the conflict was over, forty-three people had died and there were millions of dollars in property damage. Racial disturbances also broke out in Pontiac, Grand Rapids,

The Michigan National Guard controls the crowds during the race riots of July 1967.

Saginaw, Kalamazoo, and Flint in that hot summer. These occurrences caused many whites to move out of the cities, speeding the decline of major urban areas.

As a result, citizen committees realized that drastic action was needed and worked hard to create what they called a New Detroit. Through their efforts, more blacks were eventually elected to office and gained positions of authority in the state. Coleman Young, Detroit's first African-American mayor, served from 1974 to 1993.

Although it was a struggle, Michigan made great strides to come back economically in the 1980s. Industry concentrated on better products and more diversity. Banks and other lending institutions improved their efficiency. Michiganders did not want to be characterized as living in the "Rust Bowl," with collapsing companies and out-of-date technology. By the 1990s, the state had regained its footing and was poised to look forward into the next century. Companies such as Kmart, headquartered in Troy, and Domino's Pizza, based in Ann Arbor, may be the business wave of tomorrow for Michigan.

Tax Breaks Given

Empowerment zones, areas created within cities to encourage industrial development, were established. In these projects, companies were given tax breaks to locate in metropolitan areas. The state's scientific brainpower continued to develop wonderful new ideas that contributed to growth. One inventor was even working on a way to use cherry waste by-products to make meatless hamburgers!

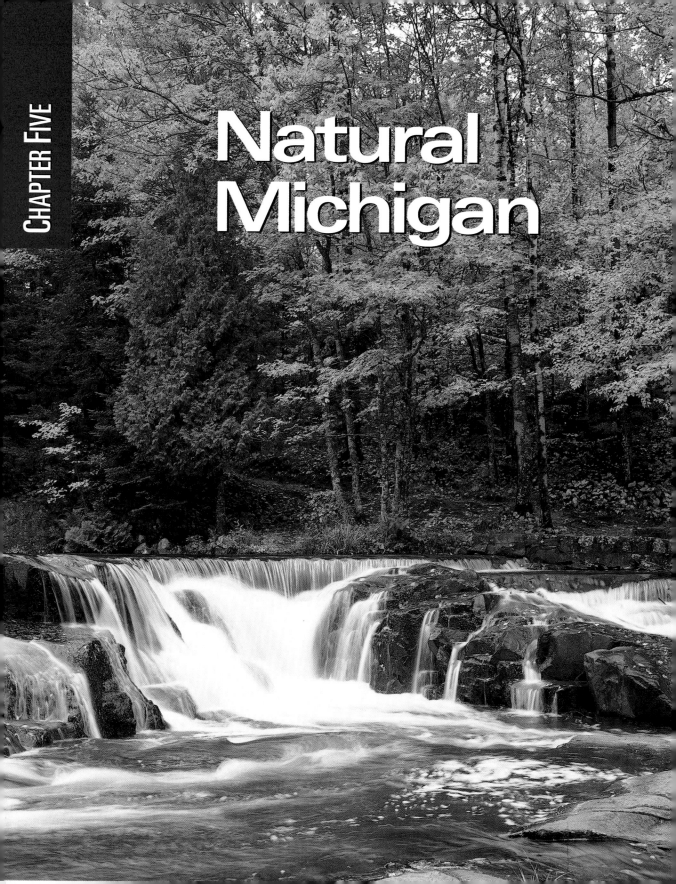

CHAPTER FIVE

Natural
Michigan

Michigan is the only state separated into two distinct parts. The northern part of Michigan is called the Upper Peninsula, and the southern part is the Lower Peninsula, often called the "mitten" of the state because of its appearance. The little peninsula north of Detroit is considered the "thumb" of the mitten. The peninsulas are separated by the Straits of Mackinac, a passage that links two of the Great Lakes—Huron and Michigan. The Soo Locks, at the city of Sault Ste. Marie, allow freighters to travel from Lake Huron to Lake Superior. The Mackinac Bridge spans the straits, allowing motorists to travel back and forth from Upper to Lower Michigan. The southern border of the Upper Peninsula touches northern Wisconsin, while the southern border of the Lower Peninsula sits atop Indiana and Ohio. A stretch of the Upper Peninsula touches Canada's Ontario province, as does the Detroit River in the Lower Peninsula.

Mackinac Island, with Fort Mackinac seen on the bluff.

Opposite: Bond Falls

Mackinac Island

The Straits of Mackinac have always been important to the development of North America's midsection. Native Americans and early adventurers knew the value of the straits, which served them like a highway intersection during that era. The French and British had trading posts there, and explorer Father Jacques Marquette established a shoreline mission at the village of St. Ignace in 1671. His body is now buried at the Marquette Mission Park and Museum of Ojibwa Culture.

Midway across the straits lies Mackinac Island, which can be reached only by ferryboat and small plane. No automobiles are allowed on the island, so horse-drawn wagons and bicycles carry visitors around. It is fun to climb to the top of the walls of the reconstructed Fort Mackinac, an imposing battlement high on the bluffs overlooking the straits. Although once briefly captured by the British, the fortress played an important role in defending the young United States during the War of 1812.

Today, a tourist town nestles beneath the bluffs. Stores there sell delicious fudge and souvenir T-shirts. Beyond the town is a wooded area of oaks and pine trees. An 8-mile (13-km) road circles the rugged interior of the island, taking travelers to Sugar Loaf, a high limestone rock, and Arch Rock, a natural bridge along a lakeside cliff.■

Michigan Measurements

Michigan is 455 miles (732 km) long and 400 miles (644 km) wide. The state's 58,513 square miles (151,548 sq km) anchor the north-central United States. Today's landscape was created 9,500 to 15,000 years ago, during the last great Ice Age.

Just as there are two distinct geographical sections of Michigan, there are also two major land formations. The Superior Uplands are the most dramatic, rearing their craggy heads high over the western half of the Upper Peninsula. The Uplands rise 600 to 1,980 feet (183 to 604 m) high. The Porcupine Mountains are the most prominent landmass. This vast blanket of rock is topped by Mount Curwood, the highest point in the state at 1,980 feet (604 m) above sea level.

The Great Lakes Plains provide another striking landscape. Their rolling hills, sand dunes, and farmland stretch along the eastern portion of the Upper Peninsula and make up the Lower Peninsula.

Valuable Minerals

Copper and iron are among the valuable mineral deposits in Michigan. Petroleum, limestone, salt, and gypsum are also present. The state's large deposits of sand, clay, and gravel are important for the construction industry. The U.S. Bureau of Mines estimates that Michigan's production of nonfuel minerals ranks fifth among the states. Michigan is also among the top fifteen states in the production of oil and gas.

The Michigan Department of Environmental Quality emphasizes that it is important to understand Michigan's geology. Such knowledge not only promotes the wise use of resources, but also protects groundwater and provides essential information for responsible land use.

Water Wonderland

Anyone who loves water is sure to love Michigan, which has more fresh water than any other state. Michigan has 150 waterfalls and

Hikers enjoy the Porcupine Mountains.

Lake Michigan

Michigan is named after Lake Michigan, from the Ojibwa word *michigama*, meaning "great water." Lake Michigan is the third largest of the Great Lakes and the only one entirely within the borders of the United States. The lake covers 22,400 square miles (58,016 sq km) and stretches about 118 miles (190 km) from the Straits of Mackinac to the western side of Green Bay at its widest point. The Ojibwa people, who lived in Michigan for centuries, considered the lake waters to be the sacred home of powerful spirits called the *manito*. ■

Opposite: Lake Superior, the world's largest freshwater lake

more than 11,000 inland lakes. Its 3,288 miles (5,292 km) of shoreline are the longest of any state, except Alaska. Clearly, Michigan is a great place for fishing fans, boaters, swimmers, and folks who simply love to watch the sun set over water.

Water has shaped the state of Michigan. Four of the five Great Lakes lap at Michigan's beaches, cliffsides, and sand dunes. Lakes Michigan, Huron, Erie, and Superior make up one of the largest collections of fresh water in the world. In fact, Lake Superior is the largest freshwater lake anywhere, covering 31,800 square miles (82,362 sq km).

Important Waterways

Michigan's waterways have always been important for drinking water, irrigation, recreational activities, industry, and food resources. The state has such an abundance of fresh water that it has been suggested some of it be sold. According to several plans, the water could be piped or trucked to drier states. However, not many people in Michigan look favorably on that idea!

The American Indians hunted deer as the animals came to lakes to drink. Waterfowl were brought down by slings and arrows. The Indians fished for pike and panfish, using torches at night to lure the fish to the surface. Beavers and otters provided lush fur pelts for clothing. Raspberries, elderberries, and gooseberries were tasty and nutritious.

Rivers and lakes were highways to the Native American. Sleek birchbark canoes carried goods around the region. A great web of commerce existed long before the first French explorer arrived. Following the American Indians' example, the *voyageurs* (the French

Michigan's Geographical Features

Total area; rank	96,705 sq. mi. (250,464 sq km); 11th
Land; rank	58,513 sq. mi. (151,548 sq km); 22nd
Water; rank	39,896 sq. mi. (103,330 sq km); 2nd
Inland water; rank	1,704 sq. mi. (4,413 sq km); 13th
Great Lakes water; rank	38,192 sq. mi. (98,917 sq km); 1st
Geographic center	Wexford, 5 miles (8 km) northwest of Cadillac
Highest point	Mount Curwood, 1,980 feet (604 m)
Lowest point	572 feet (174 m) along Lake Erie
Largest city	Detroit
Longest river	Grand River, 260 miles (418 km)
Population; rank	9,328,784 (1990 census); 8th
Record high temperature	112°F (44°C) at Mio on July 13, 1936
Record low temperature	−51°F (−46°C) at Vanderbilt on February 9, 1939
Average July temperature	69°F (21°C)
Average January temperature	20°F (−7°C)
Average annual precipitation	32 inches (81 cm)

Sleeping Bear Dunes National Lakeshore

The Sleeping Bear Dunes National Lakeshore in western Michigan near Empire is a desertlike expanse of sand dunes. The largest, towering 465 feet (142 m), is in the shape of a bear and gave the area its name. The dunes were formed by the last Ice Age, which filled Lake Michigan with ice. As the glaciers turned southward, they crushed all the softer rocks and created sand. As the ice melted, the lake level rose higher than it is today. The water eventually receded, leaving the sand behind. The west wind from the lake piled the sand into the dunes.

Eventually, the blowing sand cut off bays from Lake Michigan, thereby creating numerous small inland lakes. Over the centuries, much of the surrounding sand became firmer, allowing grass, shrubs, and trees to grow. But out on the windswept Sleeping Bear Point, the dunes are bare. The shifting sands prevent anything from growing on them. ◼

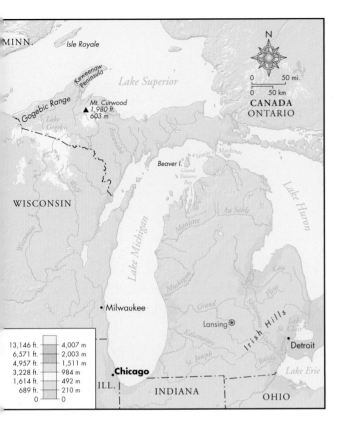

Michigan's topography

Detroit's harbor handles cargo from around the world.

trappers and traders) fanned out across the state's waterways. After them came the loggers, the settlers, and the city builders. Newcomers arrived by ferry and steamboat from points east, rather than taking the long, hard route overland. From yesterday's canoes to today's oceangoing freighters, water has helped Michigan grow.

The rivers in the Upper Peninsula have musical names, taken from lyrical American Indian dialects. The peninsula is crosshatched by the Escanaba, Manistique, Menominee, Tahquamenon, and Ontonogan Rivers. The Sturgeon and Whitefish Rivers are named for the fish found in the surrounding lake waters.

The Sturgeon

The sturgeon, the world's largest freshwater fish, may live to be more than 50 years old. It has a long history, dating back thousands of years, according to fossil evidence. The sturgeon is probably ugly to everyone but its mother with its long, skinny snout and bony armor all along its body. Four sensors, called barbels, dangle in front of its mouth and help it find food on the bottom of the lakes. Sturgeon eggs, called caviar, are an expensive gourmet treat. ■

Rivers in the Lower Peninsula include the Kalamazoo, Saginaw, Muskegon, Au Sable, Raisin, and St. Joseph. The Grand is the longest river in Michigan, flowing westward from the center of the state for 260 miles (418 km) to empty into Lake Michigan. On the eastern side, the wide Detroit River links Lake Erie to Lake St. Clair, which then connects with Lake Huron. Ships and barges can easily get to Detroit.

The water wonderland of Michigan is home to many species of fish. You can cast a line into any stream and hope to catch a brook trout, or go out on the choppy waters of Lake Michigan to chase salmon. Michigan is rightly proud of its record catches. One of the largest was a muskie weighing almost 48 pounds (21.6 kg). The 51.5-inch (131-cm) fish was caught in Clam Lake in 1985. Bass, perch, crappies, and catfish also live in these waters. Towns along the eastern shore of Lake Michigan are important harbors for Michigan's large fishing fleet.

Michigan's Wild Side

The wild side of Michigan is home to bears, rabbits, raccoons, mink, weasels, squirrels, deer, and, at last count, 500 moose that weigh more than 1,000 pounds (450 kg) each. Bird species range from pheasants to finches. In 1997, the state's annual bald eagle survey counted 853 sightings, the highest level in nineteen years,

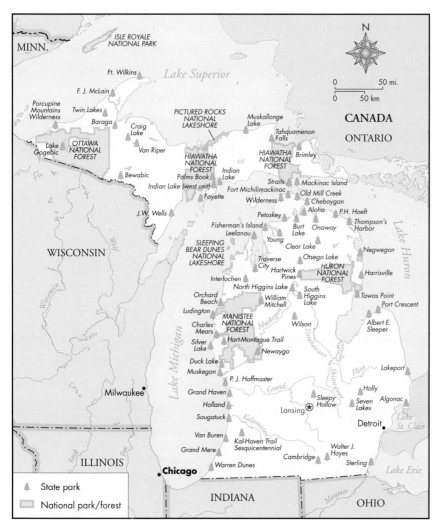

Sugar maples in
Ottawa National Forest

Michigan's parks and
forests

The map includes the following labels:

MINN.

ISLE ROYALE
NATIONAL PARK

Lake Superior

CANADA

ONTARIO

Ft. Wilkins

F. J. McLain

Porcupine
Mountains
Wilderness

Twin Lakes

Baraga

Craig Lake

PICTURED ROCKS
NATIONAL
LAKESHORE

Muskallonge
Lake

Tahquamenon
Falls

Lake Gogebic

OTTAWA
NATIONAL
FOREST

Van Riper

HIAWATHA
NATIONAL
FOREST

HIAWATHA
NATIONAL
FOREST

Brimley

Bewabic

Palms Book

Indian
Lake

Mackinac Island

Indian Lake (west unit)

Straits

Old Mill Creek

WISCONSIN

J. W. Wells

Fayette

Fort Michilimackinac

Cheboygan

Wilderness

Aloha

P.H. Hoeft

Petoskey

Fisherman's Island

Burt
Lake

Onaway

Thompson's
Harbor

Leelanau

Young

Clear Lake

SLEEPING
BEAR DUNES
NATIONAL
LAKESHORE

Traverse
City

Otsego Lake

Negwegon

Hartwick
Pines

HURON
NATIONAL
FOREST

Harrisville

Interlochen

North Higgins Lake

South
Higgins
Lake

Orchard
Beach

William
Mitchell

Tawas Point

Ludington

MANISTEE
NATIONAL
FOREST

Wilson

Port Crescent

Charles
Mears

Albert E.
Sleeper

Silver
Lake

Hart-Montague Trail

Newaygo

Duck Lake

Muskogon

Lakeport

P. J. Hoffmaster

Milwaukee

Grand Haven

Sleepy
Hollow

Holly

Algonac

Holland

Lansing

Seven
Lakes

Saugatuck

Detroit

Lake
St. Clair

Van Buren

Kal-Haven Trail
Sesquicentennial

Walter J.
Hayes

Grand Mere

Cambridge

Sterling

Chicago

Warren Dunes

Lake Erie

ILLINOIS

INDIANA

OHIO

Maumee

State park

National park/forest

Lake Michigan

Lake Huron

0   50 mi.
0   50 km

N

Natural Michigan **59**

Isle Royale

Isle Royale, Michigan's only national park, peeks above the choppy cold waters of northwestern Lake Superior. It lies 20 miles (32 km) from the Minnesota mainland and 48 miles (77 km) from the Upper Peninsula. The park includes the main island and about 200 tiny islets, none of which is inhabited. Isle Royale has America's largest herd of moose, as well as a pack of wolves. You can reach the main island only by ferryboat. ■

including 63 sightings of our majestic national bird soaring high over Gogebic County.

Timber Resources

Trees are another abundant resource. The state has 19.3 million acres (7.8 million ha) of timber, ranking fifth among the states. Economists value these trees at $12 billion. More than 200,000 people make a living from the forests. Although most of the timber is privately owned, there are six state forests in Michigan and ninety-nine state parks and recreation areas. There are also three national forests—the Ottawa, Hiawatha, and Huron-Manistee.

State Timber

Most of the denser forests stand in less populated northern Michigan. More than 90 percent of the Upper Peninsula is timbered. Hard maple and birch are the most plentiful trees, but pine, oak, hickory, elm, ash, and soft maple are also common. The scientific term for these trees is broadleaf *deciduous*, meaning they change with the seasons. They are spectacular in autumn, when the leaves change colors. The logged trees are made into many products, from bookshelves to houses.

The major softwoods, called *coniferous* (meaning they bear cones), are red, white, and jack pines, spruce, fir, and northern white cedar. These trees are easily identified because of their ever-green needles. They are often decorated for Christmas and used in the making of paper.

Forests act as an air-filtration system. By releasing oxygen, the trees help keep the air clean. Acid rain from industrial and automotive pollution damages the trees. Forest workers are always on the lookout for insects or diseases that kill trees and for fires that can destroy the entire landscape.

Forest Fires

Although federal, state, and local fire-fighting agencies work closely together to prevent or limit forest fires, the state records some 8,500 fires each year. From 10,000 to 12,000 acres (4,000 to 5,000 ha) of forest are destroyed by fire annually. While most fires are small and easily extinguished, some cause widespread destruction. In 1986, twenty-four fires burned more than 7,000 acres (2,800 ha) in Marquette County in a single afternoon. One fire forced the evacuation of 8,000 workers from the K. I. Sawyer Air Force Base. In 1990, the Stephan Bridge Road Fire near Grayling burned 6,000 acres (2,400 ha). Almost 100 homes and other buildings were destroyed as well.

One of the problems facing Michigan is the number of people who build their homes in remote parts of the state. Many homeowners do not allow enough open space as a firebreak around their houses. More than 600,000 houses were built in remote northern Michigan in the 1980s alone. This increase of human activity in areas of highly flammable forestland increases the danger of fire. There are other problems as well. Smaller budgets and fewer fire-

Fire!
A forest fire can spread rapidly. Danger is especially high when the temperatures are 60°F (15°C) or higher, the relative humidity is only 15 to 30 percent, and winds are 15 miles (24 km) per hour or more. This combination causes an explosive situation, especially in dry jack pine forests where 20 acres (8 ha) can burn in fifteen minutes. ■

fighters make it increasingly difficult for the state's Department of Natural Resources to guard the more than 20 million acres (8 million ha) under its protection.

Environmental Consequences

All this construction has other environmental consequences as well. Plants and animals are directly affected by the sprawling growth of Michigan's communities, as well as by pollution and erosion. State officials work hard to maintain healthy natural areas on public and private lands. Since 1972, twenty areas totaling 48,081 acres (19,458 ha) have been officially designated as wilderness, wild, or natural areas. Some of these natural areas are havens for endangered wildlife such as the black bear and gray wolf. An endangered species is any fish, plant, or animal that is in danger of extinction throughout all of its territory. Other endangered Michigan species are perhaps less well known. They include a fish called the creek chubsucker, insects such as the American burying beetle, and plants such as the dwarf milkweed. Michigan environmentalists are concerned that many natural wonders will be lost forever if they are not protected now.

Temperate Climate

The weather in Michigan is generally moist and temperate—a boon to farmers. The Upper Peninsula is usually colder in winter than the Lower Peninsula. In January, temperatures range from 10° to 25°F (–12° to –4°C) in Escanaba, while it is 19° to 32°F (–7° to 0°C) in Detroit. In July, the weather is very pleasant throughout the state, ranging from 58° to 75° F (14° to 24°C) in Escanaba and 63° to 84° F (17° C to 29° C) in Detroit.

At least six out of every ten days in summer are partly cloudy. The year's annual precipitation (moisture from rain and snow) ranges from 26 to 36 inches (66 to 91 cm). Snow in the Upper Peninsula is often piled high over the roofs of garages. This is because of fierce storms that sweep in from the west over Lake Superior. Snowplows and shovels are part of everyday life from November to April. Yet, on the fun side, so are snowshoes, snowboards, and skis.

A snowplow is a common sight during a Michigan winter.

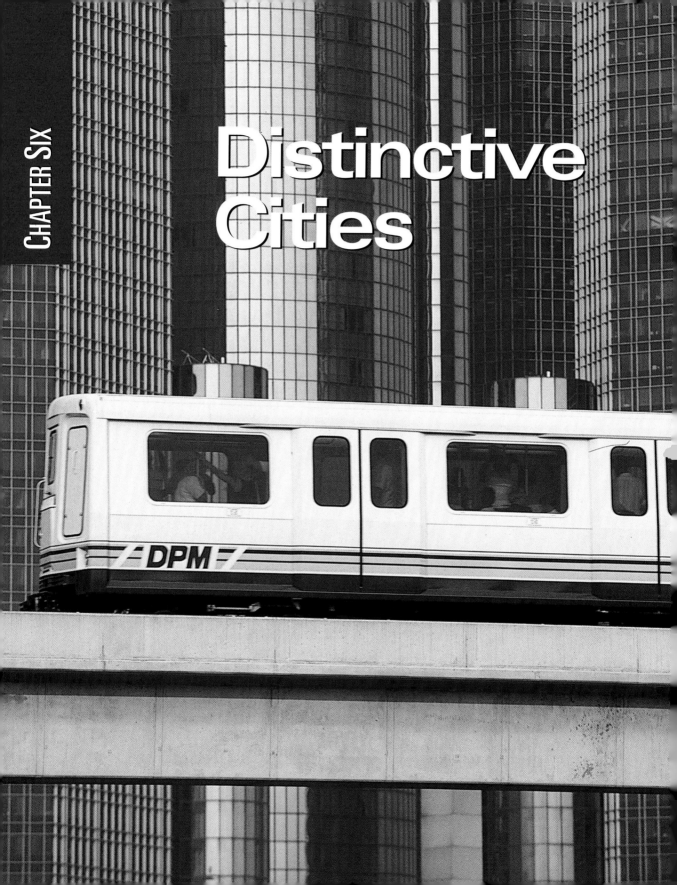

CHAPTER SIX

Distinctive Cities

Each Michigan city has its own style. Whether it's a rural crossroad or a major metropolitan area, every community has plenty of personality. Copper Harbor, the state's northernmost town, is on the far end of the rockbound Keweenaw Peninsula. An old harbor and mining town, Copper Harbor is now a summer resort on the shores of Lake Superior.

Copper Harbor in autumn

In pioneer days, nearby Fort Wilkins protected copper miners from Indian attacks. The fort stood on the shores of calm Lake Fanny Hooe, named after an officer's wife. According to legend, Fanny was so beautiful that she broke the heart of every man who saw her.

Copper Country

South of Copper Harbor is Hancock, known as the hub of the Upper Peninsula's copper country because of the rich metal found in the vicinity. After decades of intensive mining, however, the mine shafts are depleted. The community was named after John Hancock, one of the signers of the Declaration of Independence. Many Finns settled there because the forests, the lakes, and the clear blue skies reminded

Opposite: A tram in front of the Renaissance Center in downtown Detroit

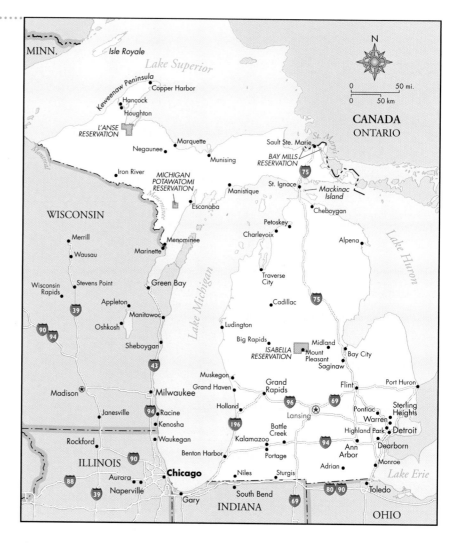

Michigan's cities and interstates

them of home. Visitors enjoy putting on hard hats and slickers to descend 1 mile (1.6 km) or more under the Earth's surface to explore the vast caverns of the Arcadian Mine. In the 1800s, the Arcadian was one of the world's largest copper mines.

Marquette

The biggest town in the Upper Peninsula is Marquette, the seat of Marquette County. Both the city and county are named after the famous missionary priest, Père Jacques Marquette. The city sits on a high cliff overlooking Lake Superior. Its 328-acre (133-ha) Presque Isle Park is one of the largest urban parks in North America. The first American flag in the area was flown at the park's Granite Point in 1820. Marquette's location made it an ideal harbor. In the past, it was an important port for lake freighters hauling iron ore and timber.

Oldest Town

Sault Ste. Marie is located on the banks of St. Marys River directly across from Sault Ste. Marie, Canada. The French visited the area as early as 1618, but there were no permanent settlers until Père Marquette arrived in 1668.

Traverse City

The Ottawa, Ojibwa, and Potawatomi Indians hunted and fished in the Grand Traverse Bay region. The French trappers who gave the town its name canoed south along the west shore of Lake Michigan and came to the mouth of a large bay. They had to leave the coast to cross a spit of land and called the portage *la grande traverse* (the grand traverse). The town was incorporated as a city in 1895. The sheltered harbor was a perfect anchorage for schooners carrying pine boards and planks to Chicago, Racine, and

Olympic Training

Marquette is a sports-minded community. Northern Michigan University is a training site for twenty-three Olympic sports events. Downhill skiers love to test their skills on Marquette Mountain. They can plunge down a 600-foot (180-m) vertical drop or try any of the other sixteen runs that crisscross the sharp slope. ■

other Great Lakes ports. From these cities, Michigan's fresh lumber was hauled by wagon or train to build homes in the prairie states.

Farming eventually replaced logging around Traverse City. The soil was especially good for apples and cherries. The orchard industry did so well that Traverse City is now called the Cherry Capital of the World. The city hosts the annual National Cherry Festival, dating back to 1926 and attended by more than 300,000 people each year.

World's Biggest Cherry Pie

Pies are still popular in Traverse City. The stainless steel pie tin for the world's "biggest cherry pie" can also be seen along the Traverse City marina. The tin is 17.5 feet (5.5 m) in diameter and 26 inches (66 cm) deep. The 28,355-pound (12,862-kg) pie was baked on July 25, 1987. The pie-baking was sponsored by the National Cherry Council and Chef Pierre, Inc., a subsidiary of Sara Lee Corporation. The Sara Lee people make 12 million pies a year at their local plant. ▪

The Soo Locks

St. Marys River is the only water link between Lake Superior and the other Great Lakes. In one section of the river, the water falls about 21 feet (6.5 m) from Lake Superior to the lower lakes. This waterfall was a barrier to ships until 1797 when the first lock was constructed. By 1855, several "Soo Locks" were in use.

A lock carries a ship from one level of water to another. As water is allowed into the space between two lock gates, the vessel rises to the next level. When the water is released, the ship is lowered. The current lock system can accommodate ships that carry up to 72,000 tons of cargo. The Soo Locks help overseas products to reach their inland destinations. Iron ore, grain, machinery, and other products are mined, farmed, and manufactured in the midwestern United States and funneled back out on their way overseas. ■

Port of Entry

Saginaw is the port of entry into Central Michigan, situated on Lake Huron's Saginaw Bay. A fort was built there in 1820, and the city was chartered in 1857. Saginaw has gone through many changes over the generations. It started as a fur-trading outpost, evolved into a lumber town, and is now the center of the state's sugar beet industry.

Grand Rapids

Grand Rapids is one of Michigan's major manufacturing centers. Located on the roaring Grand River, the city built the first hydro-

Fabian Fournier

Legendary Paul Bunyan (shown above in a cartoon, lifting a tree over his shoulder) is the giant lumberman of myth and the focus of many tall tales. Yet he may have been based on the real exploits of a Saginaw timberman. Fabian (Saginaw Joe) Fournier was known for his wood-cutting skills and his great strength. Fournier was among thousands of men who worked the woods in the late 1800s and early 1900s. They used to come to town to party and rest up for more work in the forests. The toughest of the tough were the "river rats," jumping from log to log in their heavy hobnail boots. They rode the timber rafts down the wild Saginaw River to Saginaw's sixty sawmills. To protect their carpets, hotel keepers made the lumbermen wear slippers when they stayed overnight. ▩

electric plant in the Midwest during the late 1800s. Since 1838, furniture-making has been one of Grand Rapids' major industries. Calling the city their home are five of the world's largest office-furniture manufacturers. Sofas and chairs are made in Grand Rapids, as are grandfather clocks. The Howard Miller Clock Company makes more of these traditional timepieces than any other manufacturer in the world.

Other major employers are automaker General Motors, home-care-product manufacturer Amway, and Wolverine World Wide, which makes Hush Puppies shoes. The Gerald R. Ford Museum, opened in 1997, displays the papers and memorabilia of hometown boy and thirty-eighth U.S. President Gerald Ford.

Flint

Another major auto center is Flint, the "Vehicle City." In its earliest years, Flint was known for its quality horse-drawn carriages, and it then began to make "horseless" carriages. But the city's first automaker, the Flint Automobile Company, produced only fifty-two cars in two years and went out of business at the turn of the century. Next came

Billy Durant, David Buick, Louis Chevrolet, and Dallas Dort, whose cars were much more popular. Today, the General Motors plant in Flint makes luxury vehicles and trucks.

Roads to Lansing

All roads in Michigan seem to lead to Lansing, the state's capital city. The city was named after John Lansing, an American Revolutionary War hero. When the town was first laid out in 1847, the state legislature considered other names. Among those considered were Michigan, Pewanogowink, Swedenborg, and El Dorado. The name of Lansing won out. Construction of the current state capitol building lasted from 1871 to 1879. It was designed by Elijah E. Myers, one of America's foremost architects, and renovated in the 1990s.

The city hosts a ten-day Michigan Festival each year, featuring artists, craftworkers, and performers from around the state. The main program includes a Children's Festival. Young people can enjoy special shows and participate in hands-on art activities. That event is one of several that make Lansing the state's Festival Capital. There is also an African-American Cultural Festival, the Car/Capitol Celebration, the East Lansing Art Festival, the Mexican Fiesta, Michigan Parades into the 21st Century, and Riverfest. Silver Bells in the City, a celebration of the city's arts scene, is held on the weekend before Thanksgiving.

Detroit's metropolitan area covers more than 2,026 square miles (5,247 sq km) and is home to about 4 million people. About 1 million citizens live in the city itself. The urban community encompasses Wayne, Oakland, and Macomb counties. Long known

The Labor Museum

The Labor Museum in Flint is the only museum in Michigan dedicated to the history of working men and women. Exhibits trace the union movement from before statehood to the present. There is a display about the mid-1930s sit-down strike at the city's General Motors Plant, illustrating the difficulties in getting decent working conditions for autoworkers. The GM workers occupied the plant until the company agreed to their demands. ■

The capitol in Lansing

Olds Motor Works

In 1897, Lansing native Ransom Eli Olds formed the Olds Motor Works, Michigan's first operating automaker. The city celebrated the 100th anniversary of the company in 1997 with festivals, art shows, and parades. ■

as the Automobile Capital of the World, Detroit is also home to more than 1,000 other major corporations. Antoine de la Mothe Cadillac, who started a fur-trading center there in 1701, would never have dreamed his tiny village would have grown so much. The city was incorporated in 1815 and was the capital of Michigan for a brief time before that honor passed to Lansing.

Many Firsts

Detroit and the surrounding area have many "firsts." In 1869, it became the first city to assign individual telephone numbers. The world's first convention bureau was organized here in 1896, and the world's first concrete highway opened there in 1908. Henry Ford instituted the first assembly line in Detroit in 1913, revolutionizing

industry. The nation's first shopping mall opened in suburban Southfield in 1954. Coleman Young was elected Detroit's first black mayor in 1973. In 1994, the Pontiac Silverdome hosted the first indoor soccer championship in World Cup history. The play-offs of the World Cup, the world's most popular sporting event, are watched by millions of viewers every four years.

Detroit has many other interesting and odd things to call its own. It has the only floating post office in the world. It is the only major city in the continental United States that lies north of the Canadian border. It shares the first traffic tunnel between two nations—the Detroit-Windsor Tunnel. It is one of the largest ports in the United States, carrying almost 30 million tons of cargo each year.

The Detroit skyline, seen from Windsor, Ontario

A street in Greenfield Village (left) and an antique Ford from the Henry Ford Museum (right)

Much of Detroit's past is showcased in the Henry Ford Museum and Greenfield Village in suburban Dearborn. The sprawling complex also contains many displays of national interest. The museum showcases entire buildings, such as a courthouse in which Abraham Lincoln practiced law, inventor Thomas Edison's laboratory, and the workshop in which the Wright Brothers developed their airplane. One entire display focuses on the automobile and how it has affected life in America.

Cereal City

The battle that gave Battle Creek its name was not much of a fight. Two members of a surveying party wrestled with two Indians on the bank of a creek in 1825. No one was hurt, but the surveyors marked "battle by the creek" on their map. So Battle Creek was the name given to a village that grew up on the site. The city was chartered in 1859. Before the Civil War, Battle Creek was nicknamed the Health City because of its spas and hospitals. But it was better known as one of the main stops on the Underground Railroad, which was a trail to freedom leading north from the Southern slave states. Today, it is the Cereal Capital of the World—the headquarters of the Kellogg Company, the Post Division of Kraft Foods, and Ralston Foods.

Best Place

Swing Magazine, a publication for the twenty-something crowd, calls Ann Arbor one of the ten best places in the country in which to live. The editors cite the community's cultural activities, job opportunities, and casual lifestyle. Ann Arbor is the home of the University of Michigan, the first state university to admit women, in 1870.

Young people are attracted to Ann Arbor because it has the largest concentration of computer software firms in the Midwest. Borders and Waldenbooks, two of the country's largest bookstore chains, are also headquartered in Ann Arbor. The city boasts more than 200 restaurants, but there is more to do in Ann Arbor than eat. Each March, thousands of Native Americans from the United States and Canada gather in Ann Arbor for a huge powwow. Singers, dancers, and artisans wear the colorful traditional clothing of numerous Indian nations.

Sojourner Truth

Sojourner Truth was a noted African-American woman and a former slave who spoke out for women's rights, abolition, and prison reform. Truth, who was born Isabella Baumfree, came to live in Battle Creek in 1856. From there, she toured the country speaking out for the poor and downtrodden. She died in 1883 and is buried in the city's Oak Hill Cemetery. A U.S. postage stamp was issued in her honor in 1986. ■

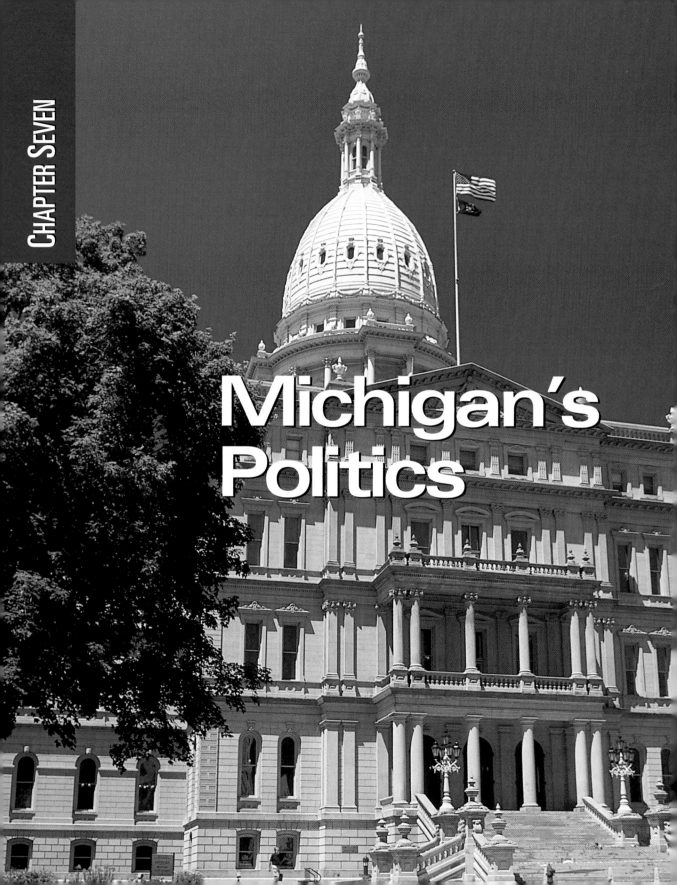

CHAPTER SEVEN

Michigan's Politics

A famous quote says that all politics are local—meaning that citizens are always concerned about what happens at their own front door. They can look out the window and see if the roads are plowed or if the garbage is picked up. If not, they simply call town hall to complain. The Michigan constitution, which was approved in 1963, allows "home rule" or self-government for local communities, encouraging participation in all levels of government. The state's cities and towns are governed by mayors and city councils or by city managers.

Michigan Governor John Engler at the 1994 National Governors' Conference in Washington, D.C.

In addition to its town governments, Michigan is divided into eighty-three local entities called counties. Sixty-eight counties are in the Lower Peninsula and fifteen in the Upper Peninsula. A county executive is usually the chief governmental officer, assisted by an elected county board of commissioners. The counties maintain facilities such as jails, courthouses, and parks. Their social service agencies look after the welfare of elders, children, and the handicapped. Other county offices include the sheriff, treasurer, attorney, clerk, and registrar of deeds.

Important Document

The Michigan constitution is modeled after the U.S. Constitution. The document lets state residents know their rights and obligations

Opposite:
The state capitol

Stevens T. Mason

At age twenty-two, Stevens T. Mason became acting territorial governor of Michigan in 1834. As acting territorial secretary at age nineteen, he had led the fight for statehood. He approved a census, one of the requirements needed to become a state, and led the convention that drew up the articles of the first state constitution.

Never one to sit back and relax, Mason went on to become governor in 1837. He served until 1840, overseeing the transition of Michigan from a territory to a full-fledged state in 1837. A state office building in Lansing as well as Mason County and a town in Ingham County, are named after this young governor. ■

as citizens. The Michigan constitution can be amended, or changed, only after approval by the state Senate and a majority of the voters. The constitution separates state authority into three branches: the executive, judicial, and legislative divisions.

The governor and lieutenant governor are elected for four-year terms. They can be elected to only two terms. The governor appoints important officials such as the state treasurer and heads of departments who make sure that Michigan functions smoothly. In riots and other emergencies, the governor can call up the state militia to keep order. The governor may also use the weekend soldiers to help direct traffic and clean up after tornadoes, floods, and other natural disasters.

The governor is the state's chief promoter, encouraging businesses to bring new jobs to Michigan. Company presidents appreciate it when the governor calls to discuss money-making opportunities, showing that Michigan really wants their business in the state. The governor is also the head of his state political party, leading a delegation to its respective national presidential convention. Except for two nineteenth-century governors who belonged to the old Whig Party, all Michigan's governors have been either Democrats or Republicans.

The judicial branch of the Michigan government interprets laws and tries cases. There are seven justices on the state Supreme Court, the highest court in the state. The justices are elected to eight-year terms and name one of their members to be chief justice. Among the state courts is an eight-member court of appeals, elected from three districts according to population. The fifty-seven circuit courts throughout Michigan are the highest trial courts in the state.

Michigan's Governors

Name	Party	Term	Name	Party	Term
Stevens T. Mason	Dem.	1837–1840	Hazen S. Pingree	Rep.	1897–1900
William Woodbridge	Whig	1840–1841	Aaron T. Bliss	Rep.	1901–1904
James W. Cordon	Whig	1841–1842	Fred M. Warner	Rep.	1905–1910
John S. Barry	Dem.	1842–1845	Chase S. Osborn	Rep.	1911–1912
Alpheus Felch	Dem.	1846–1847	Woodbridge N. Ferris	Dem.	1913–1916
William L. Greenly	Dem.	1847	Albert E. Sleeper	Rep.	1917–1920
Epaphroditus Ransom	Dem.	1848–1849	Alexander J. Groesbeck	Rep.	1921–1926
John S. Barry	Dem.	1850	Fred W. Green	Rep.	1927–1930
Robert McClelland	Dem.	1851–1853	Wilber M. Brucker	Rep.	1931–1932
Andrew Parsons	Dem.	1853–1854	William A. Comstock	Dem.	1933–1934
Kinsley S. Bingham	Rep.	1855–1858	Frank D. Fitzgerald	Rep.	1935–1936
Moses Wisner	Rep.	1859–1860	Frank Murphy	Dem.	1937–1938
Austin Blair	Rep.	1861–1864	Frank D. Fitzgerald	Rep.	1939
Henry H. Crapo	Rep.	1865–1868	Luren D. Dickinson	Rep.	1939–1940
Henry P. Baldwin	Rep.	1869–1872	Murray D. Van Wagoner	Dem.	1941–1942
John J. Bagley	Rep.	1873–1876	Harry F. Kelly	Rep.	1943–1946
Charles M. Croswell	Rep.	1877–1880	Kim Sigler	Rep.	1947–1948
David H. Jerome	Rep.	1881–1882	G. Mennen Williams	Dem.	1949–1960
Josiah W. Begole	Dem. and Greenback	1883–1884	John B. Swainson	Dem.	1961–1962
			George W. Romney	Rep.	1963–1969
Russell A. Alger	Rep.	1885–1886	William C. Milliken	Rep.	1969–1983
Cyrus C. Luce	Rep.	1887–1890	James Blanchard	Dem.	1983–1991
Edwin B. Winans	Dem.	1891–1892	John Engler	Rep.	1991–
John T. Rich	Rep.	1893–1896			

Other Courts

Every Michigan county has a probate court, which supervises wills, looks after the estates of deceased Michigan residents, and ensures that their wishes are followed. Many cities have municipal courts that oversee judgments involving minor offenses including shoplifting, jaywalking, and parking violations. All Michigan judges are elected for six-year terms.

The Capital City

Lansing, a vibrant, modern city tucked into the center of the state, has been Michigan's capital since 1847. The headquarters of most state departments and the state's capitol are in Lansing. Lansing almost didn't get the "job" as chief city. According to the state constitution of 1835, a permanent site for the capital had to be chosen within the first two decades of statehood. The legislature wanted the capital to be in the center of the state, where it could easily be reached. So Detroit was the capital from 1837 to 1847 when the legislature voted to relocate from Detroit to Ingham County's rough and rugged Lansing Township.

Early Michiganders looked at Lansing with raised eyebrows. Many thought that the site selection was a joke because nothing was there except a few frontier houses. A capital commission, however, went quickly to work. It laid out the "Town of Michigan" in 1847. An area bounded by today's Michigan and Capital avenues and Allegan and Washtenaw streets was chosen for the construction

Gerald R. Ford

President Gerald R. Ford was the thirty-eighth president of the United States. He was born on July 14, 1913, in Omaha, Nebraska, as Leslie Lynch King Jr. His parents divorced when he was two years old and his mother moved to Grand Rapids. There she married local businessman Gerald R. Ford, who adopted Leslie and gave him his name. Ford graduated from the University of Michigan in 1935, where he was an outstanding football player. He served on an aircraft carrier during World War II.

Ford was elected to thirteen successive terms in the House of Representatives as a Michigan Republican. In 1965, he became House minority leader. President Richard Nixon asked Ford to be his vice president when Vice President Spiro Agnew was forced to resign in 1973.

When Nixon stepped down from the presidency on August 9, 1974, Ford became president. He was the first U.S. president not voted into office. Then Ford was defeated in the 1976 presidential election by Jimmy Carter, a Democrat. After losing, he served on the boards of several companies and gave lectures around the country. A library holding all his papers is in Ann Arbor. ◼

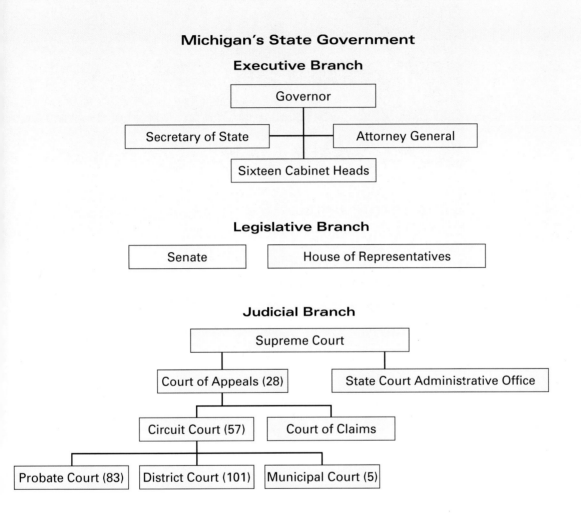

Michigan's State Government

Executive Branch

- Governor
- Secretary of State
- Attorney General
- Sixteen Cabinet Heads

Legislative Branch

- Senate
- House of Representatives

Judicial Branch

- Supreme Court
- Court of Appeals (28)
- State Court Administrative Office
- Circuit Court (57)
- Court of Claims
- Probate Court (83)
- District Court (101)
- Municipal Court (5)

of the state capitol building. When the legislature met that year, many lawmakers had to stay in the homes of private citizens because hotels had yet to be built. During the session, the legislators voted to officially rename the city as Lansing.

The city has subsequently proved itself to be a good choice. In 1993, it was called one of the country's "up and coming cities" by *City & State* magazine.

An elevated view of the state capitol rotunda

Candace S. Miller

Candace S. Miller was elected Michigan's fortieth secretary of state in 1994, becoming the first woman to hold that position in Michigan. Miller's job is an important one. After the lieutenant governor, the secretary of state is second in line of succession to the governor. And the secretary acts as governor when both of these other officials are out of the state. The secretary of state is also responsible for overseeing Michigan's motor-vehicle laws. In addition, she functions as the state's historian and serves as the chief elections official. ■

Bicameral Legislature

The Michigan legislature is bicameral, which means it is made up of two distinct groups: a Senate and a House of Representatives. There are thirty-eight senatorial districts, each with 212,400 to 263,500 residents. Elections are held in November, with senators taking office on January 1. The Senate helps draw up laws and approves appointments made by the governor.

The Michigan House of Representatives has 110 members who are elected in even-numbered years and serve two-year terms. The chief officer of the House of Representatives is the speaker, elected by members of the House.

The House meets on Tuesdays and Wednesdays when legislators can be seen hurrying through the capitol building, rushing to get to their seats by 2 P.M. when sessions begin. Their Thursday session begins at 10 A.M. Sometimes, if there is pressing legislation, the House also meets on Mondays and Fridays. Occasionally, sessions last late into the night.

Meetings, seminars, conferences, and related legislative activities take up the rest of the week. The legislature has many duties. It enacts laws, levies taxes, and oversees the actions of the governor. The governor may veto, or overrule, an act of the legislature, but the legislature can override the veto. Senators and representatives also serve on committees that supervise various functions of government, from farming to transportation. It is important for the legislators to know what is happening throughout the state, as well as in their own districts.

Bills Introduced

During a two-year session, from 4,000 to 8,000 bills are introduced. Only 600 to 800 survive the lengthy process of debate and compromise to become law. Visitors can watch legislators at work from the ornate galleries overlooking the House and Senate chambers. A record of House and Senate activities is published in journals produced daily by each body.

On a federal level, there are sixteen Michigan representatives in the U.S. House of Representatives and two senators in the U.S. Senate. These congressmembers serve their terms in Washington, D.C. They work on legislation affecting the entire country. Of course, the lawmakers from Michigan always try to serve their own constituents—the people who elected them—as best they can. For instance, a U.S. congressperson can smooth the way for government contracts to go to Michigan companies. He or she also keeps an eye on national legislation, to ensure that the elderly, the business community, the poor, and the young are protected.

Michigan's congressional delegation in Washington works for the good of the nation, as well as for the benefit of the state. For instance, in 1921, Senator Charles Townsend led the battle in Congress for the establishment of the Federal Highway Act. This piece of legislation created a countrywide network of highways.

State Flag and Seal

The current state flag was adopted in 1911. On the blue banner is a representation of the state seal, which was adopted in 1835. A bald eagle, the national bird of the United States, is in the center of the seal. It represents the superior authority of the national government. An elk on the left side of the seal and a moose on the right side represent Michigan. These animals hold up a shield with the Latin word *tuebor*, which means "I will defend."

The first Michigan flag was flown in 1837, the year Michigan became a state. It bore the state seal and depicts a soldier and a woman on one side and a portrait of Stevens T. Mason, Michigan's first governor, on the

other side. In 1865, the flag carried the state coat of arms on a field of blue on one side and the coat of arms of the United States on the opposite side. ■

Michigan State Symbols

Robin, the state bird

Petoskey stone, the state stone

Painted turtle, the state reptile

State bird: Robin The robin was selected in 1931 after winning an election sponsored by the Michigan Audubon Society.

State fish: Brook trout The brook trout was chosen in 1988 because it is such an excellent game fish. It is native to the Upper Peninsula and spread through the Lower Peninsula in the late 1900s.

State gem: Greenstone The greenstone (Chlorastolite) was made the state gem in 1972. It is sometimes called the Isle Royale greenstone because it is found in the Upper Peninsula.

State reptile: Painted turtle The painted turtle was adopted in 1995 after a group of schoolchildren in southwestern Michigan urged their legislators to support their efforts.

State tree: White pine The white pine was named state tree in 1955 because it was important to Michigan's early lumber industry.

State stone: Petoskey stone Michigan adopted the Petoskey stone in 1965. It comes from a coral reef that existed in the northern part of the Lower Peninsula millions of years ago.

State flower: Apple blossom The apple blossom has been the official flower since 1897. It was chosen because Michigan is a leading apple producer.

State soil: Kalkaska sand Kalkaska sand covers nearly 1 million acres (0.4 million ha) in twenty-nine Michigan counties. It is among the most widespread of almost 500 types of soil found within the state. It was named state soil in 1990. ■

Michigan's State Song

"Michigan, My Michigan"

There are several versions of the song, one of which was written by Winifred Lee Brent in 1863. The most commonly used words were composed in 1902 by Douglas M. Malloch.

A song to thee, fair State of mine,
Michigan, my Michigan;
But greater song than this is
*   thine,*
Michigan, my Michigan;
The whisper of the forest tree,
The thunder of the inland sea;
United in one grand symphony
Of Michigan, my Michigan.

I sing a State of all the best,
Michigan, my Michigan;
I sing a State with riches bless'd,
Michigan, my Michigan;
Thy mines unmask a hidden
*   store,*
But richer thy historic lore,
More great the love thy builders
*   bore,*
Oh Michigan, my Michigan.

How fair the bosom of thy lakes,
Michigan, my Michigan;
What melody each river makes,
Michigan, my Michigan;
As to thy lakes, thy rivers tend,
Thy exiled children to see thee
*   send*
Devotion that shall never end,
Oh Michigan, my Michigan.

Thou rich in wealth that makes a
*   State,*
Michigan, my Michigan;
Thou great in things that make
*   us great,*
Michigan, my Michigan;
Our loyal voices sound thy claim
Upon the golden roll of fame
Our loyal hands shall write the
*   name*
Of Michigan, my Michigan. ■

CHAPTER EIGHT

GENERAL MOTORS
BUILDING

1920

Michigan's Many Muscles

M ichigan has a diverse economy with three major industries—manufacturing, farming, and tourism. From 1985 to 1995, Michigan's growth was equal to or greater than the national average and employment continues to grow steadily in a wide range of

companies. This balance is important because it spreads out the economic benefits. Michigan's economy survives economic downturns because if one industry weakens, another can take its place.

Farming is among Michigan's chief industries.

Automotive Center

Michigan remains the automotive center of North America, with sales in the billions of dollars, though it is 35 percent less dependent on auto jobs today than it was in the 1980s. However, it is the auto industry that continues to keep Michigan on the business front line.

Ransom Olds turned out his first inexpensive auto in 1890, to be followed by other manufacturers. Among these early leaders was the visionary Henry Ford, who created the black Model T that sold for around $290 and changed the face of American life. Travel became easier and businesses could receive and ship goods more quickly.

The world's love affair with the car quickly took hold. For Michigan, it was a remarkably rapid expansion. To speed up the

Opposite: The General Motors building in Detroit

Automotive Firsts

Michigan has many automotive "firsts." Among them, the state boasts of laying the nation's first mile of concrete highway (1909) and installing the country's first traffic light (1915). ■

**Henry Ford and a
Model T sedan in 1920**

manufacturing process, Ford developed the assembly line, a technique used by almost every industry today.

The Big Three automakers remain among the state's largest employers, with thousands of workers. Each company has a long history in Michigan. Ford was launched in 1903, General Motors was founded in 1908, and Chrysler started in 1925. All are headquartered in the Detroit area. Today, Michigan builds 29 percent of the nation's autos and leads in light truck production. The state is home to 92 of the country's 107 automotive research and development facilities. Of the top 150 U.S. automotive suppliers, more than half are in Michigan.

What Michigan Grows, Manufactures, and Mines

Agriculture
Milk
Corn
Greenhouse and nursery
   products
Beef cattle

Manufacturing
Transportation equipment
Machinery
Fabricated metal products
Food products
Chemicals

Mining
Natural gas
Iron ore
Petroleum

Today, other Michigan industries are hard on the heels of the auto world. Chemicals, electronics, fabricated metals, printing, publishing, and rubber are growing industries. Tourism alone employs 115,000 people in accommodations, attractions, and service-related operations. This sector is expected to grow as people learn about Michigan.

Industrial Powerhouse

Michigan has been an industrial powerhouse since pioneer days. The enthusiasm and business skills of its residents have helped its businesses to grow—like its rich crops. Hard work and enthusiasm, along with a variety of available natural resources, helped many immigrants become millionaires. Irish, Finns, Arabs, Greeks, Dutch, African-Americans, Germans, and many other ethnic groups contributed to the state's strong economic scene. Their efforts usually brought success.

The arrival of Europeans changed the face of Michigan, turning it into today's potpourri of farms and forests, manufacturing plants and mills, small-town stores and urban art galleries, chain restaurants, and mom-and-pop diners. Every imaginable kind of business contributes to Michigan's economy.

Copper Mining

Mining was the first major commercial success story in the state. Thousands of years ago, Michigan's prehistoric residents used crude tools to dig for copper in the rich deposits of the Upper Peninsula. Following the lead of these Native Americans, early set-

Michigan's Inventions

Michigan inventors have always been busy. Michiganders made the first seeding machine (1840), the electric dental drill (1875), the pneumatic hammer (1890), the world's first wrecking crane (1883), the first gas-filled, lighter-than-air dirigible (1929), and the hand-operated record player (1969). ■

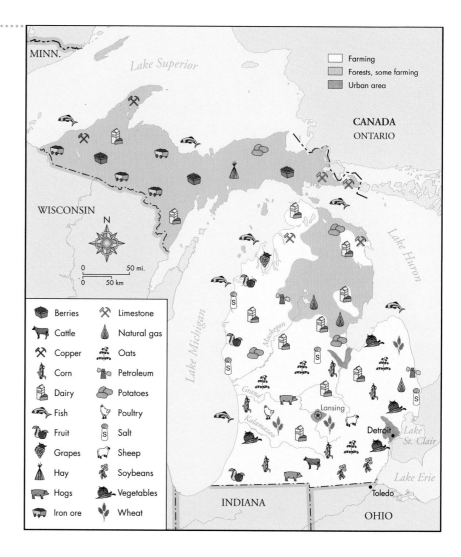

Michigan's natural resources

Map legend:

Berries	Limestone		
Cattle	Natural gas		
Copper	Oats		
Corn	Petroleum		
Dairy	Potatoes		
Fish	Poultry		
Fruit	Salt		
Grapes	Sheep		
Hay	Soybeans		
Hogs	Vegetables		
Iron ore	Wheat		

Farming
Forests, some farming
Urban area

tlers were drawn to the rough landscape of northern Michigan. Commercial copper production began in 1845 and ended in 1969, when the last of the huge copper companies closed. Labor troubles, a declining world market, and depleted resources contributed to the industry's death. During the mining heyday, a giant power shovel at Quincy Mine in Hancock could dig ten tons of copper ore out of the ground in a single scoop.

Along the ravines of the Marquette, Gogebic, and Menominee iron region, thick pine forests now surround the open pits where early miners dug for iron ore. The Michigan Iron Industry Museum in Negaunee overlooks the turbulent Carp River, on the site of the first iron forge in the Lake Superior region. From 1848 to 1855, the Jackson Iron Company and others in the region made iron products from local ore. Even with a drop in mining output because of a decline in high quality material, the state still produces 20 percent of the nation's iron ore.

Cedar logs in Ensign, Michigan, ready for shipping

The Timber Industry

Logging brought the next business boom in the state, beginning in the 1840s and lasting well past the Civil War. The lumber fueled the needs of a growing America. Timber was floated down the state's rivers to huge mills that cut the logs into planks. Once the railroads slashed their way westward, it became easier to send logs to market. Even today, Michigan has the largest variety of commercial tree species among the states.

Billions of board feet of white pine and other excellent

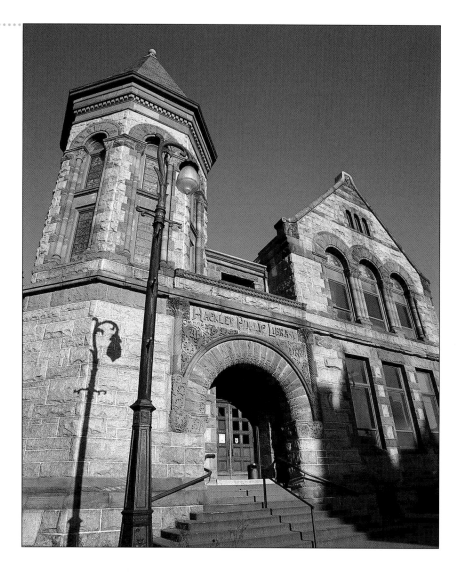

The Hackley Library
in Muskegon

woods went into buildings all across the Midwest. The great
demand quickly reduced Michigan's forest to an ugly vista of
stumps and scrub brush. One of Michigan's wealthiest timber
barons, Charles Hackley of Muskegon, did not leave the state
when the trees ran out. He foresaw the disappearance of the forests
and had already purchased timberland in the far West. Staying in
his hometown, he donated more than $6 million to build a library,

A farmer inspects his apple crop, near Grand Rapids.

park, school, and other public buildings that are still used today.

The timber industry has made a comeback in Michigan. There are 270 sawmills, 14 veneer mills, and 8 paper and pulp mills in Michigan, employing 63,000 people. More than 4 million Christmas trees are also harvested in the state each year, providing $50 million annually to the state's growers. The timber industry contributes $1.5 billion annually to the state's economy.

From Forests to Farming

The clearing of the forests allowed farmers to move in. They planted crops and started dairy farms. Michigan now produces more than seventy agricultural products. Its fields of asparagus, corn, and tomatoes seem to stretch on forever, and its 150,000 acres (60,705 ha) of orchards overflow with apples, cherries, and pears. Farming, the state's second-leading industry, contributes $37 billion to the Michigan economy each year. Corn, hay, and soybeans are the most valuable crops, totaling nearly 62 percent of Michigan's farm income. One out of every fifteen Michigan citizens is employed in the food and agriculture field, making the industry the second-largest employer in the state.

Michigan for Breakfast

A bit of Michigan is part of almost every box of breakfast cereal. Battle Creek, a city in the central part of the state, is home to the Post and Kellogg corporations, giant manufacturers of popular breakfast foods. Charles William Post (1854–1914) was a Michigan food manufacturer who developed a mix of molasses and bran. His tasty invention, called Postem, was one of the first commercial breakfast foods. From there, he went on to develop other cereal foods. William Keith Kellogg (1860–1951) (right) produced the first cornflakes. A statue of Tony the Tiger of Kellogg's Frosted Flakes fame stands outside the company's home office. ■

Agriculture Groups

As the farming industry grew more important, trade organizations were established by the Michigan legislature. They oversee and help market a diverse range of products, providing a support group for every crop. They include the Michigan Apple Committee, the Michigan Grape and Wine Industry Council, the Michigan Asparagus Advisory Board, and the Michigan Fresh Market Carrot Committee.

What Michigan Produces

Michigan residents like their homegrown goodies. Michiganders buy 25 percent of the beef, 60 percent of the pork, 25 percent of the lamb and mutton, 60 percent of the turkey, and 66 percent of the eggs the state produces.

But each year, Michigan also exports, or sends, goods valued at $2 billion to other countries. In 1994, a peak year for shippers, growers sent $77 million worth of fruit and $158 million worth of vegetables to other countries. While these exports are good for all farmers, overseas sales are especially important to the bean growers.

The Michigan Bean Commission points out that every other row of beans planted in the state is sold outside the United States. Various types of beans are preferred by different nationalities. Italians and Spaniards like yellow-eyed beans. Cooks in northern Mexico enjoy pinto beans, while those in the south like black beans.

When it is summer north of the equator, it is winter south of the equator. The equator is an imaginary line that divides the world into the Northern and Southern Hemispheres. Countries south of the equator love Michigan's fresh fruit because it arrives on their store shelves in the months when their own produce does not grow. For instance, Brazilians enjoy munching Michigan's crimson Delicious apples.

Canning Companies

Companies specializing in canned and dried vegetables are also important to Michigan's economy. The Eden Food Company, one of America's largest producers of organic foods, works directly with farmers who do not use chemical fertilizer or pesticides on their crops. Eden sells its products around the United States and in Canada.

All the tart cherries produced in the state are made into other food products. If you like cherry pie, it is likely that the filling comes from Michigan. Dried cherries are also sold as snack foods.

Adzuki Beans

Japanese people buy all the adzuki beans that Michigan can produce. To serve this market, Michigan farmers plant from 4,000 to 7,000 acres (1,600 to 2,800 ha) of adzukis every year. These little red beans are used to make *anko*, a sweet paste used in cooking and baking. The Japanese like the Michigan crop because it is so similar to the beans grown in Japan. ■

Sweet Chips

Chips from cherry trees have a sweet, smoky aroma that makes them perfect for barbecues. The Traverse Fruit Wood Company in Traverse City provides cherry, apple, hickory, and sugar maple chips for such diverse clients as the U.S. Culinary Olympic Team and the World Champion Barbecue Team. ■

Because Michigan is first in the nation in the production of blueberries, a large percentage of that crop is turned into juice, dried fruit, and pie filling. European, Japanese, and Caribbean grocery stores stock these products on their shelves.

One Michigan product grows well in the dark. More than 17 million pounds (8 million kg) of mushrooms are harvested annually. They are raised in special buildings with temperature and humidity controls. To preserve freshness, the mushrooms are on grocery store shelves within twenty-four hours of picking.

Harvesting cherries is big business.

Michigan Cherry Pie

Cherries are one of Michigan's largest crops and Michigan has been home to record-breaking giant-size pies. Here is a delicious recipe to make at school or home.

Ingredients:

2 16-oz cans of unsweetened tart Michigan cherries
1 cup of granulated sugar
3 tablespoons of instant tapioca
1/2 teaspoon of almond extract
2 tablespoons of butter
2 9-inch pie crusts

Directions:

Preheat oven to 400°F (204°C).

Drain cherries and discard the juice.

Mix cherries, sugar, tapioca, and almond extract in a large bowl. Pour mixture into one 9-inch pie shell. Place small pieces of butter here and there on top of the cherry mixture.

Roll out the other pie crust and place on top of the cherry mixture. Use your fingers to join the edges of the top crust to the edges of the bottom crust. Use a knife to make wide, leaf-shaped slits in the top crust so that steam can escape while the pie is baking. Alternatively, cut the pastry for the top crust into thin strips to make a latticework top crust for your pie.

Bake for 45–55 minutes or until crust is a golden brown.

Allow to cool for at least an hour before serving.

CHAPTER NINE

People Potpourri

Former president and Michigan native Gerald R. Ford said he was lucky to have grown up in Michigan. He was glad to be from a state with a great cross section of national and racial characteristics. "The diversity in religion, race, and ethnic background exposed me to the world itself," he pointed out.

Children on the playground at the Friends School in Detroit

The 1990 U.S. census tallied 9,328,784 people living in Michigan. Almost 75 percent of the population live in towns of more than 2,500 residents. The larger communities are in the southern half of the state. The remaining 25 percent of the people live in Michigan's rural areas. The country folks who live in the Upper Peninsula (or the UP) are proud to call themselves Yoopers. That word has an interesting progression—from UP to Yoo-Pee to Yooper.

Ancient People in Michigan

People lived in Michigan at least 11,000 years ago. We know this because archaeologists found their broken stone tools, a spearpoint, and animal bones at a site near Flint. These early visitors were hunters who followed wild game northward as the glaciers melted

Opposite: A farmer checks an organic corn patch in Chelsea, Michigan.

An Ojibwa chief

in the last Ice Age. Over the next 4,000 years, people came and went through what is now Michigan. Shallow pits can still be seen in the Upper Peninsula where they dug for copper. One group of prehistoric Michiganders, the Hopewellians, settled down and raised crops. They buried their dead in mounds. Eventually, this culture was replaced by the ancestors of today's Native American nations.

Tribal traditions indicate that the Ojibwa, also called the Chippewa, were the most numerous Native Americans in Michigan. They traded with their neighbors, the Ottawa and the Potawatomi, in a loose alliance called the Three Fires. Another small band of Native Americans, the Menominee, lived along what is now the border between Wisconsin and Michigan's Upper Peninsula. These various tribal groups were identified by the first French explorers when they came to the Michigan territory in the early 1600s. There was no single concentration of Native American family groups in early Michigan.

Europeans Arrive

The French were the first white Europeans to enter Michigan. Coming from the north and east, they paddled down the mighty St. Lawrence River. The French colonized, trapped, and traded as they

moved deeper into the wilderness. The first European to reach St. Marys River in Michigan was Étienne Brulé in 1620. Over the years, he was followed by priests, woodsmen, and settlers. A number of cities in Michigan trace their origins to these first French adventurers. For instance, Detroit began as a small outpost, built by Antoine de la Mothe Cadillac. From these humble beginnings, modern Michigan was born.

According to the census, 96 out of every 100 Michiganders were born in the United States. Of the more than 350,000 Michigan residents born in foreign countries, the majority are from Canada. Today's Michiganders can trace their heritage to more than 100 different ethnic groups. German, Polish, and Irish are among the most numerous. Another 13.9 percent of the population is African-American, with Native Americans making up less than 1 percent.

A rising population of Asians and immigrants from the Middle East can be found in Detroit. But their arrival is not new. Although Temple B'nai Israel in Muskegon is one of Michigan's smallest

Antoine de la Mothe Cadillac on an expedition in 1683

Samuel Pokagon

Samuel Pokagon (1830–1899) was a Potawatomi leader born in Michigan's southwestern Berrien County. He was highly educated and wrote magazine articles, poetry, and books about his Native American background. He was a good friend of President Abraham Lincoln and visited him often in the White House. ■

Members of Detroit's Arab Community

Jewish congregations, it is still going strong. The synagogue was founded in 1889 by lumber merchants. In 1919, the first mosque for Muslims in the United States was built in Highland Park. The mosque still accommodates the spiritual needs of the Arabic-speaking automotive workers at the nearby Ford Rouge plant in Dearborn. By 1973, Detroit had the largest Arab community in the country.

Immigrants Lured by Jobs

Many immigrants came to Detroit in the early 1900s. Lured by the prospect of high-paying jobs, they flocked to jobs in the mills and factories. Many were skilled workers who had learned their trade in Europe. Others quickly picked up the skills necessary to make a good life in the New World. Serving the social needs of all these people were hundreds of organizations. They helped people find jobs, tutored children after school, hosted dances, and generally kept their community alive and functioning. Local churches were also the center of daily life, with services conducted in a familiar language. All this gave recent arrivals a sense of well-being while they adjusted to their new surroundings.

Not all the migration came from outside the United States. Thousands of African-Americans, along with struggling white families from such southern states as Alabama and Mississippi, came to Michigan in the 1930s and 1940s. They were looking for high-paying work and quickly filled in gaps in the assembly lines. This great internal migration of Americans mingled with descendants of previous newcomers from overseas. Aided by the influx of labor and a worldwide demand for its industrial goods, Michigan's economy soared.

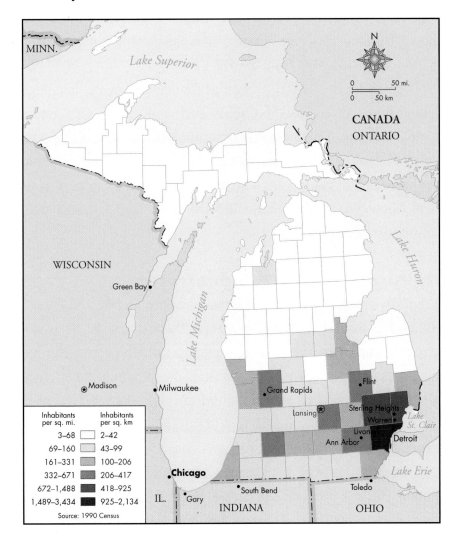

Michigan's population density

However, racial and ethnic problems developed as diverse groups competed for work. The poorer whites were afraid that African-Americans would take their jobs. Foreign arrivals, with their different customs and languages, were also suspect. While this situation has eased somewhat, tension still flares. For instance, in the 1970s and 1980s, Asians were sometimes harassed or beaten in cities that produced automobiles. Some workers, complaining about the number of cars coming from Japan, took out their frustration against anyone from the Far East.

Almost for protection, as well as for convenience in language and customs, entire neighborhoods such as Detroit's Greektown were made up of people of one nationality. Sometimes, almost entire towns shared a common ancestry. There is no question about the homeland of many folks who live in the trim, tidy town of Holland, Michigan. They celebrate their Dutch heritage with an annual tulip festival.

Culture Proudly Demonstrated

Ethnic events give everyone the chance to proudly wear folk costumes and display their music, dance, theater, and art. Detroit's African World Festival draws more than a million people to enjoy the arts, cultural displays, and activities. Frankenmuth's Oktoberfest is reminiscent of a giant autumn festival in Munich, Germany. There is even a Norwegian Pumpkin Rolling Festival in the Scandinavian town of Williamsburg!

Some cultures promote their heritage in even greater detail. Suomi College in Hancock draws students of Finnish descent from all over the world. At the picturesque campus in the pine-cov-

Detroit's Greektown

ered Upper Peninsula, courses are offered in Finland's language and culture. Detroit's Museum of African-American History opened in 1996. This marvelous complex showcases contributions of black Americans to the state and nation. It is one of the world's largest museums dedicated to the black experience.

Move to the Cities

In the mid-1800s, some 85 percent of all Michigan residents worked in agricultural jobs. Barely 100 years later, only 5 percent of the state's citizens were farming. Between World War I and World War II, Michigan was on the fast road to becoming an urban state, meaning that most of its citizens lived in cities rather than on farms. They were lured to the metropolitan areas by jobs and the high costs of farming.

Lightly Populated

Today, only about 300,000 people, barely 3 percent of the population, live in the Upper Peninsula. Marquette, with its 22,000 residents, is the largest city in the far north of the state. Farms and villages are spread far apart. However, in southern Michigan, people seem to be everywhere. Urban sprawl links Detroit and Lansing in a long corridor of shopping centers and housing tracts. Grand

Mary A. Mayo

In the 1800s, women were expected to stay home and take care of the children. However, Mary A. Mayo (1845–1903) was a strong advocate for women's education and equal rights. She was a farmer's wife at a time when it was hard for women in rural areas to get together to talk about common problems. They were isolated from each other because of the distance between farms.

In the late 1800s, an organization called the Grange helped bring people together to speak out for better working conditions on farms and to emphasize education for farm families. Mayo was inspired by the Grange and traveled the state giving speeches on the importance of recognizing women's talents. She did all this while raising a family and helping her husband. Her audiences nicknamed her "Mom Mayo" because she was so warmhearted and outgoing. Mayo even convinced the state to open Michigan's agricultural college to women students. ■

The Gerald R. Ford Museum in Grand Rapids

Michigan's counties

Detroit	1,027,974
Grand Rapids	189,126
Warren	144,864
Flint	140,761
Lansing	127,321
Sterling Heights	117,810
Ann Arbor	109,592
Livonia	100,850
Dearborn	89,286
Westland	84,724
Kalamazoo	80,277
Southfield	75,728
Farmington Hills	74,652
Royal Oak	65,400

Contrasting Populations

The combined populations of Wayne, Macomb, and Oakland counties, all in Michigan's far southeastern corner, are larger than the entire population of thirty-six states! But on the other hand, eleven Michigan counties have fewer than 10,000 people. ■

Rapids, Ann Arbor, Warren, Flint, Livonia, Dearborn, and Sterling Heights are other major urban areas. Each of these cities has a population of more than 80,000. About 80 percent of Michiganders live in these large communities.

Education Considered Important

Education has always been a priority for Michiganders. Learning was a way to get ahead. When Michigan was under British control in the 1700s, schools were established in all the garrison towns. After the Revolutionary War, teachers went from school to school. Many were ministers who conducted church services when they were not in the classroom. One of the first "official" schools in the state was opened in Detroit in 1801 by a Protestant minister. But it soon closed because the city's majority were Catholic French residents who would not send their children there.

In 1817, the first plan for an extensive public education system was drawn up by Judge Augustus Woodward. His program included classes from the lower grades through college. It was to be supported by taxes and was not affiliated with any religious group. Woodward also promoted low tuition, to give everyone the opportunity to learn. These ideas, refined and perfected by other educators over the years, formed the basis for today's strong school system in Michigan.

Schools were so small in those early years that all the grades were in the same room. In a way, this was helpful. The older children could help the younger ones with their studies. The teacher was usually an unmarried woman, sometimes only seventeen or eighteen years old. If she married, she left her job because she was then expected to stay home and raise a family. Reading, writing, and arithmetic were emphasized. Most children went to school for only a few years because their help was needed on the family farm or in the family business. Today, Michigan children between the ages of six and fifteen must attend school.

Leading the Way

The first state constitution stressed the importance of education and Michigan has led the way ever since. The state can claim credit for many firsts. It was the first to approve free high schools and the first to name a superintendent of public instruction. Eastern Michigan University in Ypsilanti, established in 1849, was the first state teachers' college west of New York. Founded in 1855, Michigan State University was the first public college in America to offer agricultural courses for credit. That was particularly important for a state like Michigan, which still considers farming to be one of its most important businesses. Michigan State was also the nation's first land-grant college. In the 1800s, the federal government reserved land in several states so that these colleges could be established.

Today, there are more than 2 million students enrolled in Michigan schools. This includes 1.7 million pupils in elementary and high school. Of those students, only ten percent attend private schools, most of which are affiliated with the Roman Catholic

Education has always been important in Michigan, even in a one-room schoolhouse.

The Plant Science and Horticulture Building at Michigan State University

Church. There are almost 720,000 college students attending the state's thirteen public universities and twenty-nine community and private colleges. The wooded campus of Michigan State University in East Lansing is the largest of these, with 41,545 students. Of this number, 2,700 come from 120 foreign countries, primarily from the Far East, including Taiwan and Korea.

This great mix of educated people forms the solid base that makes Michigan such a forward-looking state. Their contributions in science, arts, industry, agriculture, and the environment are important on both the local and national scene. That wealth of talent forms the underpinning for the state's strong, secure future.

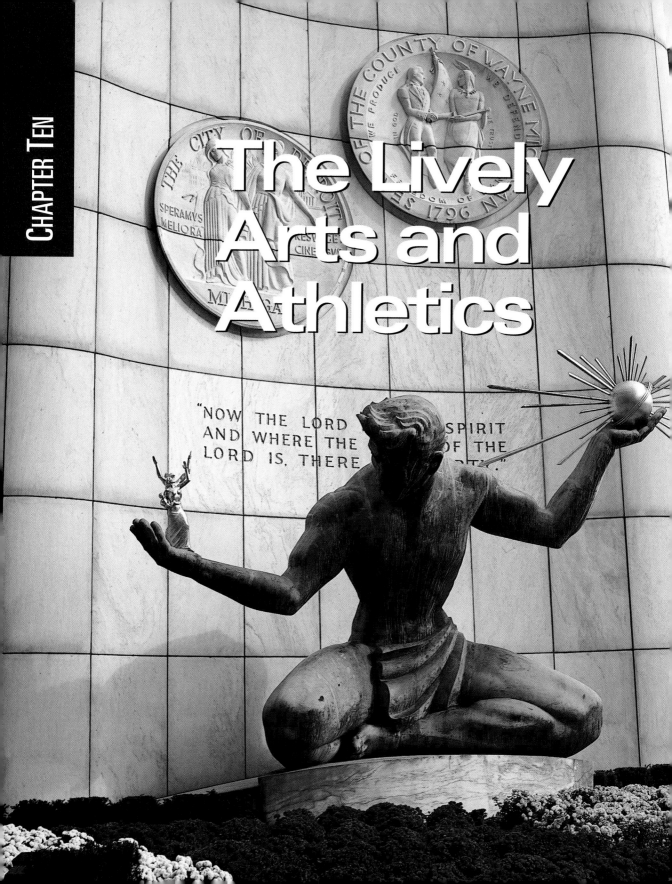

CHAPTER TEN

The Lively Arts and Athletics

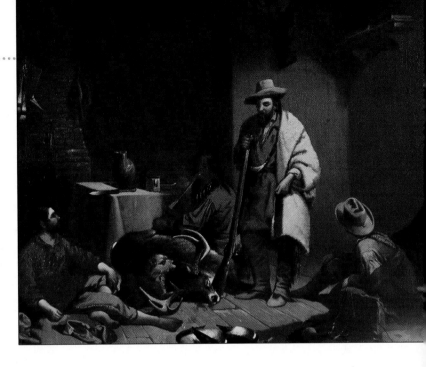

Hunters and Traders by J. M. Stanley

Michigan's artistic and cultural side continues to flourish. Painters, sculptors, dancers, poets, actors, writers, and other creative people are found everywhere. Michigan's story is told in *The Michigan Play* at the BoarsHead Theater in Lansing. The show's songs and stories about the state are accompanied by rollicking fiddle and banjo tunes.

This is certainly nothing new. Artists were working in Michigan as far back as the frontier era. J. M. Stanley traveled around the state in the 1830s. In addition to painting on canvases, he painted on the sides of buggies, carts, and farm wagons. Gildersleeve Hurd was another artist. He drew country scenes on the inside walls of houses.

Some artists roamed the state looking for work. Their wagons were loaded with paint, brushes, and ready-to-go canvases. Imagine how much work it must have taken to clip-clop down dusty or muddy roads in those days. Yet there were ways for the artist to save time and expenses and keep the cost low for the person sitting for a portrait. A settler could select a prepainted "body," choosing from several types of clothing and backgrounds. The artist would then simply paint in the face. This setup is similar to the photo shops at some amusement parks, where you can be photographed wearing "old-time clothes."

Opposite: *Spirit of Detroit* by sculptor Marshall Fredericks

James O. Lewis

The first known professional artist in Michigan was James O. Lewis. He was a printer and engraver who lived in Detroit in 1824. As part of his job, Lewis produced portraits of many famous early Michigan residents, such as territorial Governor Lewis Cass. He and Cass also designed the state seal.

Lewis was also an explorer who went on several mapmaking expeditions. On these trips, he drew portraits of the Indians who lived in the state. Many of his works were stored at the Smithsonian Institution in Washington, D.C. Unfortunately, a fire in 1865 destroyed most of his pieces. Only a few rare copies of his once-extensive portfolio remain. ▨

Vibrant Art Scene

The art scene in Michigan is vibrant and varied. Almost every large city has a museum and several galleries. There is even a Michigan Artrain, a "gallery" that tours the United States on four railroad cars, showing the work of the best state artists. Works by modern painters can also be seen on the Internet. Lowell Boileau was one of the first artists in Michigan to have his own website.

Michigan artists come from many backgrounds. Gilda Snowden is an associate professor of fine art at the Center for Creative Studies College of Art and Design in Detroit. Her visionary abstract paintings, such as *Tornadoes*, have been featured in solo and group exhibitions from Las Vegas to Nashville. In 1994, she represented the state at the Biennial National Black Arts Festival in Atlanta. As curator of exhibitions for the Detroit Repertory Theater, Snowden works with emerging artists. She has written detailed essays on the art of African-American women.

Theater History

Theater also has a long, productive history in Michigan. Some of the first stage productions were presented by soldiers quartered in Detroit. Bored with the humdrum life on the frontier, the men put on amateur shows. They played the roles of both men and women because there were few females living in the rugged wilderness.

Diego Rivera

Some artists come from far away to capture the essence of Michigan. Famed Mexican painter Diego Rivera bypassed the scenic landscape to concentrate on another subject. He chose the dirty workaday world of an automobile factory. Rivera's murals (giant wall paintings) of the Ford Rouge plant of the 1930s now adorn the walls of the Detroit Institute of Arts.

Some politicians and business leaders objected to Rivera's choice of subjects because he portrayed technology as oppressive to the workers. But the Michigan art community backed Rivera and ensured that his work was preserved. The murals are now part of Michigan's rich cultural heritage. ■

One of the state's first professional theaters was erected in Detroit in 1816, on the second floor of a warehouse. By 1837, Detroit newspapers were heralding a grand array of dramatic shows.

Today, numerous amateur and professional theater companies are active throughout the state. The Grand Rapids Civic Theater is the largest community theater in Michigan and the second largest in the United States. Among its productions are two major children's shows staged each year in its home, the glorious Majestic Theater—a grand old building built in 1903. The BoarsHead Theater in Lansing is the only Equity theater in central Michigan. Equity members are all professional actors. But the BoarsHead is not the only theater in town. Dedicated drama lovers can attend the Lansing Civic Players Guild, the Riverwalk Theater, and the Spotlight Theater as well as enjoy plays put on by Lansing Community College and Michigan State University.

Musical Productions

Music has always been important for Michiganders. Folk songs were sung around the campfires of trappers and traders. Someone usually had a fiddle or a mouth harp to get everything going. As the frontier developed and life became more organized, the first churches established choirs. In 1800, the local Indians were especially entranced by the sounds coming from an organ in Detroit's St. Anne's Church. The first piano arrived in the state in 1803, pulled to Ann Arbor by a team of oxen. The local Indian leader offered to trade six ponies for the piano.

The state has come a long way since then. The Bower Theater

in Flint and Saginaw's Civic Center are tops for musical productions and concerts. Ann Arbor even has its own Michigan Theater, home to the Ann Arbor Chamber Orchestra and other music organizations.

A Literary State

It is obvious that there has never been a shortage of creative energy in the state. One of Michigan's most famous adopted sons was author Ernest Hemingway. He loved fishing and often visited Michigan to angle for lake trout and salmon, staying in Petoskey. One of his stories, "Big Two-Hearted River," had his hero fishing at Seney in the Upper Peninsula. The Michigan Hemingway Society is planning a conference to mark the centennial of Hemingway's birth in 1999.

Among the latest crop of excellent writers with Michigan ties are novelist Richard Haft and short-story writer Sarah Smith. Haft was graduated from Western Michigan University, home of the *Third Coast* literary review. Smith grew up on Magician Lake in southwest Michigan. Milford poet Tom Lynch is also an undertaker! A book of his essays, *The Undertaking: Studies from the Dismal Trade*, was published in 1997.

John Voelker

John Voelker of Marquette was a famous Michigan author. In addition to being a writer, Voelker was also a justice on the Michigan Supreme Court. His pen name (the name he used for his books) was Robert Traver. Voelker/Traver's best-known suspense novel was *Anatomy of a Murder*, which was also made into a 1959 movie (above, with actors Arthur O'Connell, left, and James Stewart). His experiences as a judge helped Voelker create his criminal characters. ■

Linda Hunt, on the shoulders of Mel Gibson, in *The Year of Living Dangerously,* 1983. Hunt won an Academy Award for her role as a man in this film.

Unique Schools

Michigan does its part in keeping all the arts fresh and alive. The Interlochen Center for the Arts is home to the Interlochen Arts Academy, the Interlochen Arts Camp, and Interlochen Public Radio. The world-renowned school is located on 1,300 acres (526 ha) near Traverse City and began as a summer camp in 1928. The Arts Academy is a boarding school for students in the ninth to twelfth grades. More than 430 young people each year study academics, musical theater, dance, visual arts, and creative writing. Each summer, the Interlochen Arts Camp has more than 2,000 schoolchildren studying the arts under the guidance of world-class teachers. Among Interlochen's famous graduates are actresses Linda Hunt, who starred in the film *The Year of Living Dangerously,* and Meredith Baxter of TV's *Family Ties.* The school's board of trustees has included famous cellist Pablo Casals and composer Aaron Copland. More than 67,000 alumni have participated in Interlochen's many programs and more than 100,000 people visit the campus annually.

The Michigan Council for Arts and Cultural Affairs works hard to promote arts throughout the state. This association provides some funding for projects managed by the 120-plus arts groups around Michigan. Such support of the arts contributes to the quality of life in Michigan. The arts are not just important for individuals, but they also help attract economic activity to a community. The council works closely with schools, libraries, churches, community groups, and local arts organizations.

There are many examples of arts groups working hand in hand with their home communities to make Michigan a better place to live. These include the Kalamazoo Institute of Arts and the Western Michigan Cherry County Playhouse in Muskegon. Children who are frightened by abusive parents or affected by drugs and street crime can express themselves through a project with the Detroit Repertory Theatre. In Benton Harbor, arts organizations helped repair a row of abandoned storefronts. The buildings now house galleries and theaters. Michigan State University even hosted a festival showcasing the arts and music of the Hmong, refugees from Southeast Asia.

Michiganders love all kinds of sports, including bicycle races.

Participation Encouraged

Visiting a gallery, listening to a concert, hearing a poet, and learning to paint can be enjoyed by anyone. Consequently, encouraging public participation in the arts and promoting art in schools are among the Michigan Arts Council's admirable goals. Working in the arts helps develop creative skills that can be used purely for enjoyment, as well as for jobs.

Michiganders also enjoy all kinds of sports, from aerobics to water polo and everything in between. There seems to be a group

Skiers can choose from fifty-seven ski resorts in Michigan.

for every interest, such as the Michigan Mountain Biking Association and the Wolverine State Horseshoe Pitchers Association. The north-central coast of Michigan is nicknamed "America's Summer Golf Capital" because of its twenty world championship courses and ten golf resorts. Many were designed by famous golfers such as Trent Jones, Jack Nicklaus, and Arnold Palmer.

Snow is no problem for Michigan sports lovers. Eight thousand miles (13,000 km) of cross-country and snowmobile tracks crisscross the state. Downhill skiers can select a slope from fifty-seven resorts. Ski flying is another exciting sport. The observation deck at the flying hill at Copper Peak is 241 feet (73 m) above the mountain's summit. A daring skier can soar more than 500 feet (152 m) after lifting off from a 490-foot (150-m) flight deck. The U.S. Ski Hall of Fame and Ski Museum in Marquette records these winter sports in its historical exhibits and library.

Sports for Everyone

Other folks jog and run. They simply enjoy the outdoors and like to stretch their legs with the Island Road Runners, the BBC Striders, or one of the state's other running clubs. Many groups sponsor meets, and Michigan competitors place high in marathons. Every autumn, Flint hosts the internationally known Crim 10-Mile Run, which draws runners from Kenya, the Ukraine, the Netherlands, Canada, and other countries, as well as from other states. Some of Michigan's speediest women runners include Megan Fitzgerald of Sterling Heights, Kathy Kubicki of Troy, Anne Boyd of Ann Arbor, and Laura Murphy of Rochester.

Many professional athletic teams call Detroit their home. The baseball, football, basketball, soccer, and hockey clubs are legendary for their championship play.

Baseball has excited Detroit fans since 1881, as the Detroit Wolverines played in the early National League for eight seasons. When the American League started in 1901, the Detroit team was a charter member along with Boston, Chicago, and Cleveland. The team changed its name to the Tigers after

Ali Hoxie

Ali Hoxie was born to board. In 1995, the eighteen-year-old Traverse City woman placed first in her age group in the U.S. Amateur Snowboard Association Nationals at Giants Ridge, Minnesota. Swooping down the slopes on her Burton Twin Tip, she went on to earn a fifth place at the International Snowboard Federation's Junior World Championship in Zakopane, Poland. When Hoxie is not snowboarding, she's playing with her Siberian husky, Nico. She is not the only one in her family interested in snowboarding. Her uncle, Ted Hoxie, manufactures half-pipes for Midwest snowboard areas. ■

Tiger Stadium

On April 26, 1896, the first baseball game was played on the site that is now Tiger Stadium. This makes "The Corner" the oldest home of pro baseball in the world. In those early years, fans who paid fifteen cents could sit on handmade "wildcat" bleachers on top of houses behind the outfield wall. The team's current stadium was opened in 1912 and underwent many expansions and renovations.

However, the club, in partnership with the city, Wayne County, and the state, is opening a new multimillion dollar stadium in 1999. The structure will be the hub of a new sports complex in the city's downtown. Costing almost $150 million, the building is expected to be one of the most expensive in sports history. ■

Ty Cobb

Tyrus Raymond (Ty) Cobb was one of the most famous baseball players in history. He was born in Narrows, Georgia, on December 18, 1886, and played in the minor leagues for a few years. Cobb then moved on to the outfield for the Detroit Tigers in 1905. He played for the next twenty-three years for the Tigers and eventually transferred to the Philadelphia Athletics. Cobb put fear into the hearts of pitchers whenever he walked out to home plate. Over his career, Cobb was at bat 11,429 times. He had 4,191 hits, 2,244 scored runs, 892 stolen bases, and a batting average of .367. With his amazing record, he was one of the first players to be inducted into the Baseball Hall of Fame in 1936. ■

sportswriter Phil Reid noted that the club's striped stockings looked like a tiger's paw.

The Detroit Tigers won the World Series in 1935, 1945, 1968, and 1984 and have played in five others. The 1997 season saw the club complete its ninety-seventh year of American League play, ranking second in most all-time league wins to the New York Yankees.

The silver-and-blue uniforms of the Detroit Lions have been an NFL fixture for decades.

Silverdome Home

The Detroit Lions football team, organized in 1934, calls the Pontiac Silverdome its home. The building seats 80,366 fans, making

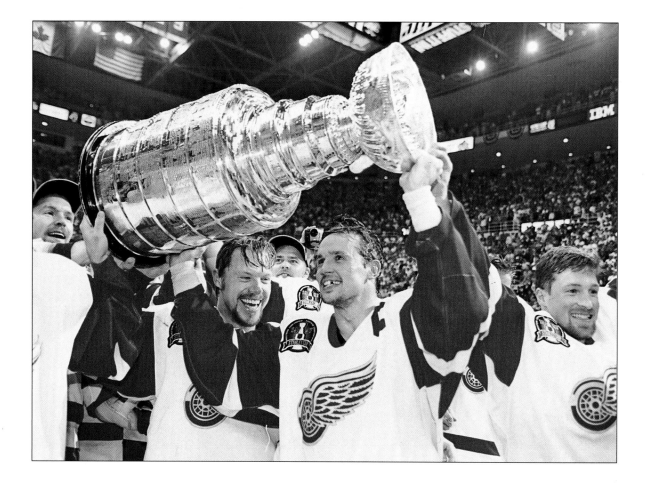

The Red Wings take home the Stanley Cup in 1997.

it the largest in the National Football League. Barry Sanders is the greatest star in Detroit Lions history. The spectacular running back tied with Brett Favre (of the Green Bay Packers) as the league MVP for the 1997–1998 season. In that season, he became only the third player in NFL history to run for more than 2,000 yards. Sanders might just be the greatest rusher in football history.

On the ice-hockey front are the gutsy Red Wings, known for their tenacious skating and scoring, especially on the ice at Joe Louis Arena. The team was formed in 1926 and went on to capture its first Stanley Cup championship by 1935. Between 1948 and

1955, the Red Wings won four Stanley Cups, the championship prize of the National Hockey League. The team finally won the Cup again in 1997, by defeating the Philadelphia Flyers. This victory ended hockey's longest championship drought, a forty-two-year shutout!

The fabled Detroit Pistons basketball team holds court in the elaborate Palace of Auburn Hills. Die-hard fans are always guaranteed plenty of action there. The Pistons' veteran guard Joe Dumars, who completed his twelfth season with the club in 1998, is highly respected for his community service off the court. He raises money for shelters, food pantries, and hospitals. His Joe Dumars Fieldhouse in suburban Detroit is a haven for Detroit's young people.

Joe Dumars, known for his basketball skills as well as for his commitment to his community

High schools and colleges throughout Michigan can boast many athletic successes. But most Michiganders reserve their greatest sports passion for the University of Michigan football team. The Wolverines are one of the most storied football programs in the nation, and decades of great play culminated with a perfect season in 1997. Michigan went 12–0 that year, beating every opponent that stood in its path. The Woverines won the Big Ten conference title, the Rose Bowl, and they shared the national championship with Nebraska. It was a season nobody in Michigan will ever forget.

Timeline

United States History

The first permanent British settlement is established in North America at Jamestown. **1607**

Pilgrims found Plymouth Colony, the second permanent British settlement. **1620**

America declares its independence from England. **1776**

Treaty of Paris officially ends the Revolutionary War in America. **1783**

U.S. Constitution is written. **1787**

Louisiana Purchase almost doubles the size of the United States. **1803**

U.S and Britain fight the War of 1812. **1812–15**

Michigan State History

1620? French explorer Étienne Brulé visits what is now Michigan.

1668 Jacques Marquette founds the first permanent settlement at Sault Ste. Marie.

1701 Antoine de la Mothe Cadillac founds what is now Detroit.

1763 The British take possession of Michigan.

1783 The United States gains Michigan from the British after the Revolutionary War.

1787 The U.S. Congress makes Michigan part of the Northwest Territory.

1800 Michigan becomes part of the Indian Territory.

1805 The U.S. Congress creates the Territory of Michigan.

1837 Michigan becomes the 26th state on January 26. Congress gives Michigan the entire Upper Peninsula.

1845 The Michigan iron-mining industry begins near Negaunee.

1854 The Republican Party is given its name at Jackson.

United States History

The North and South fight **1861–65**
ch other in the American Civil War.

The United States is **1917–18**
involved in World War I.

Stock market crashes, plunging the **1929**
United States into the
Great Depression.

The United States **1941–45**
fights in World War II.

The United States becomes a **1945**
charter member of the
United Nations.

The United States **1951–53**
fights in the Korean War.

he U.S. Congress enacts a series of **1964**
ground-breaking civil rights laws.

The United States **1964–73**
engages in the Vietnam War.

The United States and other **1991**
nations fight the brief Gulf War
against Iraq.

Michigan State History

1855 The Soo Locks is completed.

1897 Ransom E. Olds establishes
Michigan's first automobile
factory in Detroit.

1914 The Ford Motor Company establishes
a minimum daily wage of $5.

1935 Michigan workers form the United
Automobile Workers union.

1942–45 Michigan's entire automobile
industry is converted to war
production during World War II.

1957 The Mackinac Bridge is opened to
traffic between Mackinaw City and
St. Ignace.

1964 Michigan's new constitution goes into
effect.

1967 Michigan's legislature adopts a state
income tax.

1992 The Michigan Scenic Rivers Act
is passed by the U.S. Congress.
It protects more than 500 miles
(800 km) along 14 Michigan rivers
from development.

Fast Facts

Statehood document

State capitol

Statehood date	January 26, 1837, the 26th state
Origin of state name	From the Ojibwa *micigama*, meaning "great water"
State capital	Lansing
State nickname	Wolverine State, Great Lakes State, Water Wonderland
State motto	*Si quaeris peninsulam amoenam circumspice* (If you seek a pleasant peninsula, look about you.)
State bird	Robin
State flower	Apple blossom
State fish	Brook trout
State stone	Petoskey stone
State gem	Isle Royale greenstone
State song	"Michigan, My Michigan"
State tree	White pine
State reptile	Painted turtle
State soil	Kalkaska sand

Lake Michigan

Detroit skyline

Young Michiganders

State fairs	Escanaba for the Upper Peninsula (mid-August) Detroit (late August or early September)
Total area; rank	96,705 sq. mi. (250,464 sq km); 11th
Land; rank	58,513 sq. mi. (151,548 sq km); 22nd
Water; rank	39,896 sq. mi. (103,330 sq km); 2nd
***Inland water*; rank**	1,704 sq. mi. (4,413 sq km); 13th
***Great Lakes*; rank**	38,192 sq. mi. (98,917 sq km); 1st
Geographic center	Wexford, 5 miles (8 km) northwest of Cadillac
Latitude and longitude	Michigan is approximately between 41°41' and 48° 18' N and 82°7' and 90° 25' W
Highest point	Mount Curwood, 1,980 feet (604 m)
Lowest point	572 feet (174 m) along Lake Erie
Largest city	Detroit
Number of counties	83
Longest river	Grand River, 260 miles (418 km)
Population; rank	9,328,784 (1990 census); 8th
Density	159 persons per sq. mi. (62 per sq km)
Population distribution	70% urban, 30% rural

Ethnic distribution (does not equal 100%)		
White		83.40%
African-American		13.90%
Hispanic		2.17%
Asian and Pacific Islanders		1.13%
Other		0.93%
Native American		0.60%

Record high temperature	112°F (44°C) at Mio on July 13, 1936
Record low temperature	−51°F (−46°C) at Vanderbilt on February 9, 1939

A snowplow in winter

Average July temperature	69°F (21°C)
Average January temperature	20°F (−7°C)
Average yearly precipitation	32 inches (81 cm)

Michigan's Natural Areas

National Park

Isle Royale, in Lake Superior, is a forested island wilderness abundant in wildlife, including timber wolves and moose. The main island is the largest in Lake Superior. This national park comprises more than 200 islands.

National Lakeshores

Pictured Rocks, near Munising on Lake Superior, has beautifully colored cliffs carved into wonderful shapes by the waves. This was the first National Lakeshore.

Sleeping Bear Dunes, near Empire on Lake Michigan, features a mound of sand in the shape of a sleeping bear. The mound is located on a bluff about 465 feet (142 m) above the lake. This is the only national park area in lower Michigan.

Sleeping Bear Dunes

National Historical Park

Keweenaw commemorates the first significant copper mining in the United States.

National Forests

Michigan is home to three national forests: *Ottawa*, *Hiawatha*, and *Huron-Manistee*. Together they encompass 2.8 million acres (1.2 million ha) in northern Michigan along the Great Lakes.

Ottawa National Forest

State Parks

Michigan's park system is one of the largest in the United States. It has 3.9 million acres (1.6 million ha) of state forests and game areas as well as 99 state parks.

Arboretums

Leila Arboretum (Battle Creek) is a landscaped park with rare plants and a wildlife museum.

Nichols Arboretum (Ann Arbor) is home to more than 600 species of trees and shrubs, including more than 250 kinds of peonies.

Sport Teams

NCAA Teams (Division 1)

Central Michigan University Chippewas

Eastern Michigan University Eagles

Michigan State University Spartans

University of Detroit Titans

University of Michigan Wolverines

Western Michigan University Broncos

Major League Baseball

Detroit Tigers

National Basketball Association

Detroit Pistons

National Football Association

Detroit Lions

National Hockey League

Detroit Red Wings

Women's National Basketball Association

Detroit Shock

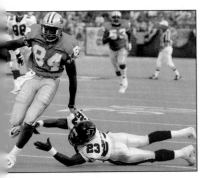
Detroit Lions

Cultural Institutions

Libraries

The Library of Michigan (Detroit) is the state library. It has collections of state and federal documents as well as collections on Michigan genealogy and law.

The Hackley Library

The William L. Clements Library (Ann Arbor), at the University of Michigan, is famous for its collections on early America.

The Gerald R. Ford Library (Grand Rapids) holds the papers of the former president.

The Detroit Public Library has several important historical collections on both the state and on Great Lakes' history.

The Walter P. Reuther Library (Detroit) is at Wayne State University. An important portion of its collections is on labor history and the Detroit region.

Museums

The Detroit Institute of Arts has a fine collection of paintings by Diego Rivera.

The Detroit Historical Museum features artifacts and exhibits on the city's history and people.

Greenfield Village (Dearborn) is a living history museum with exhibits on industry and life in the 1700s and 1800s.

The Grand Rapids Public Museum features exhibits on natural history.

Gerald R. Ford Museum

The Gerald R. Ford Museum (Grand Rapids) houses collections relating to the former president's life and administration.

The Michigan Historical Museum (Lansing) displays items dating from prehistoric times to the modern industrial era.

The Kingman Museum of Natural History (Battle Creek) has exhibits of wildlife, prehistoric mammals, and ancient relics.

The Alfred P. Sloan, Jr., Museum (Flint) features the history of transportation.

Michigan State University

Performing Arts
Michigan has three major symphony orchestras and two major opera companies.

Universities and Colleges
In the mid-1990s, Michigan had 45 public and 61 private institutions of higher learning.

Annual Events

January–March
Tip-Up Town, U.S.A. (ice-fishing festival) in Houghton Lake (January)

I-500 Snowmobile Race in Sault Ste. Marie (early February)

Invitational Nordic Ski Race in Newberry (mid-March)

Snowmobile Festival in Boyne City and Copper Harbor (mid-March)

April–July
Maple Syrup Festival in Shepherd and Vermontville (April)

Blossomtime Festival in St. Joseph–Benton Harbor (May)

Highland Festival and Games in Alma (May)

Grand Prix in Detroit (June)

Bavarian Festival in Frankenmuth (June)

Cereal Festival in Battle Creek (June)

International Freedom Festival in Detroit (late June–early July)

Lumbertown Music Festival in Muskegon (early July)

National Cherry Festival in Traverse City (early July)

Yacht Races at Mackinac Island from Chicago and Port Huron (July)

Ann Arbor Art Fair (July)

August–September
Michigan Festival in East Lansing (early August)

Upper Peninsula State Fair in Escanaba (mid-August)

Daffodils in spring

Porcupine Mountains

State Fair in Detroit (late August)

Mackinac Bridge Walk, from St. Ignace to Mackinaw City (Labor Day)

Montreux/Detroit Jazz Festival (late August–early September)

Michigan Wine and Harvest Festival in Paw Paw and Kalamazoo (mid-September)

October–December

Fall colors, statewide (October)

Red Flannel Festival in Cedar Springs (October)

Hunting season, parts of Upper and Lower peninsulas (October–November), statewide (November)

Christmas at Greenfield Village in Dearborn (December)

Famous People

President Gerald R. Ford

Avery Brundage (1887–1975)	Businessperson and sportsperson
Ralph Johnson Bunche (1904–1971)	Diplomat
Thomas Edmund Dewey (1902–1971)	Public official
Thomas Edison (1847–1931)	Inventor
Edna Ferber (1887–1968)	Author
Gerald R. Ford (1913–)	Statesman and U.S. president
Henry Ford (1863–1947)	Industrialist and philanthropist
Aretha Franklin (1942–)	Singer
Edgar Guest (1881–1959)	Writer
Lee Iacocca (1924–)	Auto industry executive
Magic Johnson (1959–)	Basketball player and business executive
William Keith Kellogg (1860–1951)	Businessperson

Joe Louis (right)

Ring Lardner (1885–1933)	Journalist and author
Charles Lindbergh (1902–1974)	Aviator
Joe Louis (1914–1981)	Boxer
Madonna (1958–)	Singer, actor, business executive
Malcolm X (1925–1965)	Civil rights activist
Pontiac (ca. 1720–1769)	Indian leader
Theodore Roethke (1908–1963)	Poet
Diana Ross (1944–)	Singer and actor
Glenn Theodore Seaborg (1912–)	Chemist

To Find Out More

History

- Brill, Marlene Targ. *Michigan*. Tarrytown, N.Y.: Benchmark Books, 1998.

- Capstone Geography Department. *Michigan*. Mankato, Minn.: Capstone Press, 1996.

- Fradin, Dennis. *Michigan*. Chicago: Childrens Press, 1992.

- Sirvaitis, Karen. *Michigan*. Minneapolis: Lerner Publications, 1994.

- Wills, Charles A. *A Historical Album of Michigan*. Brookfield, Conn.: Millbrook Press, 1996.

Fiction

- Pfitsch, Patricia Curtis. *Keeper of the Light*. New York: Simon and Schuster, 1997.

- Whelan, Gloria. *Next Spring an Oriole*. New York: Random House, 1987.

- Whelan, Gloria. *Night of the Full Moon*. New York: Knopf, 1993.

Biographies

- Cousins, Margaret. *The Story of Thomas Alva Edison*. New York: Randon House, 1997.

- Gourse, Leslie. *Aretha Franklin. Lady Soul*. Danbury, Conn.: Franklin Watts, 1995.

- Nirgiotis, Nicholas. *Thomas Edison*. Chicago: Childrens Press, 1994.

- Stanley, Jerry. *Big Annie of Calumet: A True Story of the Industrial Revolution*. New York: Crown, 1996.

Websites

- **Detroit Institute of Arts**
  http://www.dia.org/
  A virtual tour of the
  museum's collections

- **Interlochen Center for
  the Arts**
  http://www.interlochen.k12.mi.us/
  An informative guide to the
  center's many programs

- **Michigan Department of
  Agriculture**
  http://www.mda.state.mi.us/
  Complete information on
  Michigan's agricultural
  resources

- **Michigan Electronic Library**
  http://mel.lib.mi.us/
  Provides information about
  and resources for the state
  of Michigan

- **Michigan Government
  Information**
  http://info.migov.state.mi.us/
  A complete collection of
  documents and information
  about Michigan's government and history

- **Michigan Web Site
  Directory**
  http://199.190.91.5/midir/main.htm
  Wide-ranging collection of
  links to associations, educa-
  tional institutions, government, and more

Addresses

- **Library of Michigan**
  Public Services
  P.O. Box 30007
  Lansing, MI 48909
  For information about
  Michigan's industry, com-
  merce, and government

- **Michigan State Archives**
  717 West Allegan Street
  Lansing, MI 48918
  For information about Michigan's history

Index

Page numbers in *italics* indicate illustrations

abolitionists, 28
adzuki beans, 95
AFL (American Federation of
    Labor), 33–34
African-Americans, 47, 102
    Black Muslim movement, 39
    Coleman Young, mayor of
        Detroit, 49
    Cultural Festival, 71
    employment and, 42–43, *43*
    Museum of African-American
        History, 105
agriculture, 12–13, 22, *27*, 29, 33,
    68, *87*, 88, 93–96, *93, 96, 98*
    adzuki beans, 95
    cherries, 96–97
    Eden Food Company, 95
    employment in, 105–106
    The Grange, 33
    Michigan Bean Commission, 95
    trade organizations, 94
Algonquin language, 16
American Federation of Labor.
    See AFL (American Federa-
    tion of Labor).
American Indians, *18*
    Algonquin language group,
      16
    Ann Arbor powwow, 75
    Menominee, 100
    Ojibwa, 100, *100*
    Ottawa, 100
    Pontiac, 19, *19*
    Potawatomi, 100
    treaties with, 21
    waterways and, 54

animal life
    bird species, 58, 60
    black bear, 62
    gray wolf, 12, *12*, 62
    state bird, 84, *84*
Ann Arbor, 75
archaeology, 15, *15*, 99–100
art, 112–115
automotive manufacturing, 87–
    89, *88*

Bartels, Clara, 104
baseball, 121–123, *122*
Battle Creek, 74–75, 94
Battle of the Overpass, 35
Baumfree, Isabella. *See* Truth,
    Sojourner.
Belle Isle, 9, 43
board foot, 93
BoarsHead Theater, 113, 116
Boileau, Lowell, 114
borders, 12
    Great Lakes as, 10
    Upper Peninsula, 51
Bower Theater, 116–117
Brulé, Étienne, 101
    exploration route of, *18*
Brundage, Avery, 134
Bunche, Ralph Johnson, 134

Cadillac, Antoine de la Mothe, 18,
    72, 101, *101*
Cadillac Square rally, 34, *35*
de Champlain, Samuel, 16
cherries, 68, 97
Chicago Trail, 22–23

Children's Festival, 71
Chippewa. *See* Ojibwa.
Chrysler Corporation, 88
Civic Center (Saginaw), 117
Civil War, 28–29, *29*
climate, 62–63, *63*
Cobb, Tyrus Raymond (Ty), 122,
    122
Comstock, William A., governor
    of Michigan, 41
coniferous trees, 60–61
constitution, 23, 46–47, 77–78, 109
construction industry, 36–37
Copper Harbor, 65
copper mining, 27, 53, 89–90
Copper Peaks, ski flying in, 120
Coughlin, Fr. Charles, 41, *41*
Crim 10-Mile Run, 121
Custer, George Armstrong, 30

deciduous trees, 60
Department of Labor, 33
Department of Natural
    Resources, 62
Detroit, 71–74, *73*
    Detroit River, 58
    Greektown, 104, *105*
    Greenfield Village, 74
    harbor, 57
    Lions (football team), 123–124
    Museum of African-American
        History, 105
    Pistons (basketball team), 125
    Pontiac Silverdome, 73
    Purple Gang, 37
    Renaissance Center, 9, *64*

Tigers (baseball team), 121, 123
Dewey, Thomas Edmund, 134
Drinan, Fr. Robert, 23

Eastern Michigan University, 109
economy, 29–32, 87. *See also*
    employment.
    empowerment zones, 49
    Great Depression, 37, 39–40
    mining industry collapse, 46
    post–World War II, 44
    tourism, 89
Eden Food Company, 95
Edison, Thomas, 134
education, *99*, 108–111, 109, *109*
Eighteenth Amendment, 37
elections, 82
employment, *32, 34, 37*, 40, 104.
    See also economy.
    AFL (American Federation of
        Labor), 33
    African-American, 42–43, *43*
    in agriculture, 105–106
    Cadillac Square rally, 34, *35*
    construction industry, 36–37
    Department of Labor, 33
    effect of Great Depression on,
        39–40
    immigration and, 104
    International Typographical
        Union, 32
    Knights of Labor, 33
    National Brotherhood of Loco-
        motive Engineers, 32
    printer's union, 31–32
    tourism and, 89
    United Auto Workers, 35
empowerment zones, 49
Engler, John, governor of Michi-
    gan, 77
Erie Canal, 22
Executive Branch (of govern-
    ment), 77–78, 81

Famous people, 134–135
Federal Highway Act, 83

Ferber, Edna, 134
flag, 84, *84*
Flint, 70–71
    Bower Theater, 116–117
    Crim 10-Mile Run, 121
    General Motors, 71
    Labor Museum, 71
Flint Automobile Company, 70
Ford, Gerald R., 80, *80*, 99, 134
Ford, Henry, 72–74, 87–88, *88*
forest fires, 61, *61*
Fort Mackinac, 51–52
Fort Pontchartrain, 18
Fournier, Fabian "Saginaw Joe,"
    70
France, colonization by, 100–101
Franklin, Aretha, 134
Fredericks, Marshall
    Spirit of Detroit, 112
fur trade, 18–19, *20*

General Motors, 88
General Motors Building, *86*
World War II and, 42
geography
    Mount Curwood, 52
    Porcupine Mountains, *53*
    Superior Uplands, 52
Gerald R. Ford Museum, 70, *107*
government, 46, 78–83
    Candace S. Miller, secretary of
        state, 82
    constitution, 23, 46–47, 78
    county executives, 77
    elections, 82
    Executive Branch, 77–78, 81
    Federal Highway Act, 83
    Frank Murphy, 39–40, 42
    "home rule," 77
    House of Representatives, 82–
        83
    Judicial Branch, 78–79, 81
    Legislative Branch, 81–83
    Republican Party, 29
    Senate, 82–83
    State Capital building, *76*

Steven T. Mason, territorial
    governor of Michigan, 23, 78
William A. Comstock, gover-
    nor of Michigan, 41
Grand Rapids, 69–70
    Civic Theater, 116
    Gerald R. Ford Museum, 70,
        107
    Howard Miller Clock Com-
        pany, 70
Grand River, 58
Grande Traverse Bay, 67
Grange, The, 33
gray wolf, 12, *12*, 62
Great Depression, 37–40, *39*
Great Lakes, 10, 22, 54–55, 60
Great Lakes Plains, 53
Greektown, 104, *105*
Greenfield Village, 74
Guest, Edgar, 134

Hackley, Charles, 92
Hackley Library, *92*
Hancock, 65–66
Hemingway, Ernest, 117
Henry Ford Museum, 74, *74–75*
"home rule" governing, 77
Hooker, John Lee, 44, *44*
House of David, 28
House of Representatives, 82–
    83
Housewives League, 39
Howard Miller Clock Company, 70
Hoxie, Ali, 121
Hunt, Linda, 118, *118*
Hunters and Traders (J. M. Stan-
    ley), *113*
Huron National Forest, *9*

Iacocca, Lee, 134
Ice Age, 15
immigrants, 102–104
Indians. *See* American Indians.
Interlochen Arts Camp, 118
Interlochen Center for the Arts,
    118

International Typographical Union, 32
iron mining, 27, 53, 91
Isle Royale, 60, *60*
Israelites. *See* House of David.

Johnson, Magic, 134
Judaism, 101–102
Judicial Branch (of government), 78–79, 81

Kalamazoo Institute of Arts, 119
Kellogg, William Keith, 94, 134
King, Dr. Martin Luther, Jr., 47–48, *47*
Knights of Labor, 33
Knudsen, William S., 42

labor unions, 31–34
Lake Erie, 10
Lake Fanny Hooe, 65
Lake Huron, 10
Lake Michigan, 10, 54
Lake Superior, 10, 54–55, 60
Lansing, 71–72, *72*, 81
    African-American Cultural Festival, 71
    as Automobile Capital of the World, 72
    BoarsHead Theater, 113, 116
    Children's Festival, 71
    Michigan Festival, 71
    Michigan State University, 110–111
    as state capital, 80
Lardner, Ring, 135
Lee, Robert E., 30
Legislative Branch (of government), 81–83
Lewis, James O., 114
Lindbergh, Charles, 135
Louis, Joe, 40, *40*, 135
Lower Peninsula, 51, 58
Lynch, Tom, 117

Mackinac Bridge, *26*, 45, *45*, 51

Mackinac Island, *51*, 52
Madonna (pop vocalist), 135
Majestic Theater, 116
Malcolm X, 48, 135
manufacturing, 88–89
maps
    agriculture, *90*
    census, *103*
    cities, *66*
    elevation, *57*
    geopolitical, *11*
    mining, *90*
    population, *107*
    state parks, *59*
    territorial, *22*
marine life, 58, *58*, 62
Marquette, 66
Marquette, Fr. Jacques, 17–18, 52
Marquette Mountain, 68
Mason, Steven T., territorial governor of Michigan, 23, 78
Mayo, Mary A., 106
Menard, René, 17
Menominee tribe, 100
Michigan Artrain, 114
Michigan Bean Commission, 95
Michigan Cherry Pie recipe, 97
Michigan Council for Arts and Cultural Affairs, 118–119
Michigan Department of Environmental Quality, 53
Michigan Festival, 71
Michigan Iron Industry Museum, 91
"Michigan, My Michigan" (state song), 85
Michigan State University, 109–111, *110*
Miller, Candace S., secretary of state, 82
mining industry, 27, 33, 88–90
    collapse of, 46
    copper, 53
    Hancock (copper country), 65–66
    iron, 27, 53, 91

Republic Iron Mine, *27*
U.S. Bureau of Mines, 53
Model T automobile, 87, *88*
Motown Records, 44
Mount Curwood, 52
Murphy, Frank
    as governor of Michigan, 42
    as mayor of Detroit, 40–41
Museum of African-American History, 105
music, 116–117
    Bower Theater, 116–117
    Civic Center, 117
    John Lee Hooker, 44, *44*
    "Michigan, My Michigan" (state song), 85
    Motown Records, 44
Muskegon
    Hackley Library, *92*
    Temple B'nai Israel, 101
    Western Michigan Cherry County Playhouse, 119
Muslim religion, 102
Myers, Elijah E., 71

National Brotherhood of Locomotive Engineers, 32
National Guard, 48, *48*
Native Americans. *See* American Indians.
Nicolet, Jean, 16–17
    exploration route of, *18*
North Country Scenic Trail, 10
North Michigan University, Olympic Games and, 67
Northwest Ordinance, 23
Northwest Territory, 21

Ojibwa, 100, *100*
Olds Motor Works, 72
Olds, Ransom Eli, 72
Olympic Games, North Michigan University and, 67
Ottawa National Forest, *59*
Ottawa, 100

Peck, Fanny, 39
Penobscot Building, *38*
people, 13. *See also* Famous
    people.
    African-Americans, 39, 42–43,
        47, 71, *98*, 102, 105
    education of, *99*, 108–111, 109,
        109
    French, 100–101
    in Ice Age, 15
    immigrants, 31, 102
    Native American, 16
    population of, 106
Pistons (basketball team), 125,
    125
plant life, 12, *13. See also* agricul-
    ture; timber industry.
    daffodils, 8
    dwarf milkweed, 62
    state flower, 84
Pokagon, Samuel, 101
Pontiac, chief of the Ottawa,
    19–20, *19*, 135
Pontiac Silverdome, 73
population, 106–108
    contrasts in, 108
Porcupine Mountains, 9, *53*
Post, Charles William, 94
Potawatomi, 100
Presque Isle Park, 67
printers' union, 31–32
Prohibition, 37
Purple Gang, 37

Red Wings (hockey team),
    124–125
religion, 28, 39, 101–102
Renaissance Center, 9, *64*
Republic Iron Mine, *27*
Republican Party, 29
Reuther, Walter, 35
Revolutionary War, 20
Richard, Fr. Gabriel, 23, 74
Rivera, Diego, 115
rivers, 57–58
Roethke, Theodore, 135

Roosevelt, Franklin Delano, 41
Ross, Diana, 135

Saginaw, 69, 117
Sault St. Marie, *17*, 67
Schoolcraft, Henry Rowe, 22, *22*
Seaborg, Glenn Theodore, 135
Senate, 82–83
Seven Years' War, 19
skiing, 120, *120*
slavery, 28–30
Sleeping Bear Dunes National
    Lakeshore, 9, 56
Snowden, Gilda, 114
Soo Locks, 51, 69, *69*
Spain, invasion by, 20
Spirit of Detroit (Marshall Freder-
    icks), *112*
sports, 119–124, *119, 120*
    Ali Hoxie, 121
    baseball, 121
    Crim 10-Mile Run, 121
    golf, 120
    Lions (football team), 123–
        124
    in Marquette, 68
    Pistons (basketball team), 125
    Red Wings (hockey team),
        124–125
    skiing, 120, *120*
    Tiger Stadium, 121
    Tigers (baseball team), 123
Stanley, J. M.
    Hunters and Traders, 113
Straits of Mackinac, 16–17, 51–52
Sturgeon River, 57
Suomi College, 104
Superior Uplands, 52

Temple B'nai Israel, 101
theater, 114, 116–119, *118*
Tiger Stadium, 121
timber industry, 60, 91–93, *91*
    board foot, 93
    Charles Hackley and, 92
    coniferous trees, 60–61

deciduous trees, 60
forest fires, 61, *61*
state tree, 84
Traverse Fruit Wood Company,
    95
Tornadoes (Gilda Snowden), 114
Traverse City, 67–68, *68*, 95
Truth, Sojourner, 75, *75*

U.S. Bureau of Mines, 53
Underground Railroad, 28
*The Undertaking: Studies from
    the Dismal Trade* (Tom
    Lynch), 117
United Auto Workers, 34–35
University of Michigan, 75
    Museum of Art, 9
    Wolverines (football team),
        125
Upper Peninsula, 23, 25–27,
    51–52
    climate in, 63
    collapse of mining industry in,
        46
    population of, 106
    rivers in, 57
Upper Tahquamenon Falls, 10, *10*

Valley of the Giants, 9
Vietnam War, 47
Voelker, John, 117, *117*

War of 1812, 21, *21*, 52
waterways, 54
Western Michigan Cherry County
    Playhouse, 119
Whitefish River, 57
wildlife. *See* animal life; plant
    life.
Wolverines (football team), 125
Woodward, Augustus, 108
World War I, 36, *36*
World War II, 42

Young, Coleman, mayor of
    Detroit, 49

Meet the Author

Martin Hintz has written more than a dozen books for Children's Press, in both the America the Beautiful and the Enchantment of the World series. He is a member of the Society of American Travel Writers and other professional journalism societies and feels fortunate that his work allows him to visit numerous countries and states as part of his job. His bags are always packed so he's ready to go, with passport and camera in hand.

Hintz currently lives on Milwaukee's East Side, about a block from Lake Michigan. This gives him the opportunity to swim eastward across the wide lake to the state of Michigan if he wishes. As of yet, he has not attempted that feat, although he has regularly taken the car ferry from Wisconsin to Michigan and back again.

Hintz has visited Michigan many times to seek out the best cherry pie and to ski cross-country, watch migrating birds, sample bear stew, angle for lake trout, climb the sand dunes, and explore the state's wonderful cities. Augmenting his on-the-scene research, Hintz has read many library books on the state and its workings. The Internet was also a valuable resource. This is his second book on Michigan.

Photo Credits

Photographs ©:

Allsport USA: 124 (Robert Laberce), 125
Allsport/Hulton Deutsch: 40, 135
Andre Jenny: 6 top left, 72
Archive Photos: 44 (Frank Driggs), 122
Archives of Labor and Urban Affairs, Wayne State University: 35, 37, 43
Brown Brothers: 34
Corbis-Bettmann: 17, 22, 32, 39, 70
Culver Pictures: 21, 36, 100
Detroit Public Library, Burton Historical Collection: 23, 29 (Tom Sherry), 78
Doris Van Buskirk: 15
Envision: 97 (David Bishop)
Eric R. Berndt: 63
Courtesy of Ford Archives, Henry Ford Museum, Dearborn, Michigan: 88
Gamma-Liaison: 12 (Daniel J. Cox)
H. Armstrong Roberts, Inc.: cover (T. Algire), 7 top right, 112 (R. Kord)
Hulton Getty/Tony Stone Images: 30
International Stock Photo: 86, 105 (Cliff Hollenbeck)
Jim West: 6 top right, 9, 99, 115, 129 bottom
Joe Jackson: 7 top center, 92, 119, 132 top
Mark E. Gibson: 38, 69, 87, 91
Martin Hintz: 7 top left, 51, 74 left, 120, 129 top
Michigan Travel Bureau, Lansing MI: 57
National Geographic Image Collection: 60 (Phil Schermeister)
North Wind Picture Archives: 14, 18, 19, 20, 27, 101
Photo Researchers: back cover (James L. Amos), 8 (Alan L. Detrick), 133 bottom (Alan L. Detrick), 10 (Lowell Georgia)

Photofest: 117, 118
Reuters/Archive Photos: 123 (Bryan Mitchell), 131 bottom (Bryan Mitchell)
Reuters/Corbis-Bettmann: 77
Ross Frid: 68
State Archives of Michigan: 24, 109, 128 top
Stock Boston: 102 (Tony O'Brien)
Stock Montage, Inc.: 75
Superstock, Inc.: 113
Sygma: 80, 134 bottom (Allan Tannenbaum)
T.C.C.V.B.: 96
Tom Buchkoe: 67
Tom Stack & Associates: 6 top center, 45 (John Gerlach), 58 (Tom Stack)
Tony Stone Images: 55 (Glen Allison), 50, 65 (Raymond G. Barnes), 64 (D.E. Cox), 84 bottom, 131 top (Bill Ivy), 73, 82, 129 center (Vito Palmisano), 93, 98 (Andy Sacks), 26, 53 (Phil Schermeister), 2, 59, 130 bottom, 134 top (Larry Ulrich)
Unicorn Stock Photos: 13, 110, 133 top (Chris Boylan), 56, 76, 107, 128 bottom, 130 top, 132 bottom (Andre Jenny), 6 bottom, 84 top (Ted Rose), 7 bottom, 74 right, 75 left (Dennis Thompson)
University of Michigan Library, Ann Arbor, Michigan: 33
UPI/Corbis-Bettmann: 41, 42, 47, 48, 94
Visuals Unlimited: 84 center (Ross Frid), 61 (Science/VU).

Maps by XNR Productions, Inc.